REVOLUTIONARY PENNSYLVANIA SERIES

Murder at Killbuck Island

JOHN L. MOORE

Mechanicsburg, PA USA

Published by Sunbury Press, Inc.
Mechanicsburg, Pennsylvania

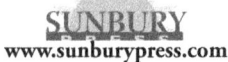

www.sunburypress.com

Copyright © 2020 by John L. Moore.
Cover Copyright © 2020 by Sunbury Press, Inc.

Sunbury Press supports copyright. Copyright fuels creativity, encourages diverse voices, promotes free speech, and creates a vibrant culture. Thank you for buying an authorized edition of this book and for complying with copyright laws by not reproducing, scanning, or distributing any part of it in any form without permission. You are supporting writers and allowing Sunbury Press to continue to publish books for every reader. For information contact Sunbury Press, Inc., Subsidiary Rights Dept., PO Box 548, Boiling Springs, PA 17007 USA or legal@sunburypress.com.

For information about special discounts for bulk purchases, please contact Sunbury Press Orders Dept. at (855) 338-8359 or orders@sunburypress.com.

To request one of our authors for speaking engagements or book signings, please contact Sunbury Press Publicity Dept. at publicity@sunburypress.com.

FIRST SUNBURY PRESS EDITION: June 2020

Set in Adobe Garamond | Interior design by Crystal Devine | Cover by Lawrence Knorr | Edited by Lawrence Knorr.

Publisher's Cataloging-in-Publication Data
Names: Moore, John L., author.
Title: Muder at killbuck island / John L. Moore.
Description: First trade paperback edition. | Mechanicsburg, PA : Sunbury
Press, 2020.
Summary: In this fifth volume of the Revolutionary Pennsylvania series, author John L. Moore covers Benjamin Franklin, Tories, General Howe, Yorktown, and murder at Killbuck Island, based on journals and other writings from the period.
Identifiers: ISBN 978-1-62006-301-9 (softcover).
Subjects: HISTORY / United States / State & Local / Middle Atlantic | HISTORY / United States / Revolutionary Period.

Product of the United States of America
0 1 1 2 3 5 8 13 21 34 55

Continue the Enlightenment!

Dedication

For Joseph W. Burns, an old and dear friend who has always encouraged my writing.

Other books in the
Revolutionary Pennsylvania series:

Against the Ice: The Story of December 1776

Tories, Terror, and Tea

Scorched Earth: General Sullivan and the Senecas

1780: Year of Revenge

Contents

Acknowledgments vii

Author's Note........................... ix

May 1775: Benjamin Franklin returns 1

July 1776: Disarming Tories................ 11

Summer 1777: Second-guessing General Howe................................ 21

January 1782: Robbing the rebels........... 31

May 1781: From York to Yorktown 45

Summer 1776: Prisoners of war 74

March 1782: Murder at Killbuck Island...... 93

Selected Bibliography.................... 115

About the Author....................... 117

Acknowledgments

Jane E. Moore and Robert B. Swift read the manuscript and suggested improvements. Jane and Robert accompanied me on visits to many of the places mentioned in the narrative. Claire Winder Kyllingstad earned a special mention by providing information about a distant uncle, Moses Winder, who appears in the chapter titled Robbing the Rebels.

About the cover

The War Party is a painting by Andrew Knez Jr.

Author's Note

I approach the many stories of the American Revolutionary War as a history-minded journalist. My mission lies in presenting the soldiers and civilians of the Revolution in their own words and in a way that lets modern readers experience a sense of immediacy with people who lived during the 1770s and 1780s. To accomplish this, I draw on soldiers' journals, letters, memoirs, and other first-person sources.

I have occasionally omitted phrases or sentences from quotations and have employed an ellipsis (. . .) to indicate where I have done so. In some instances, I have modernized spelling and punctuation.

John L. Moore
Northumberland, Pennsylvania
June 2020

May 1775
Benjamin Franklin returns

Events in Boston had a steady impact on events in Philadelphia and London.

The Boston Tea Party, held in December 1773, featured Massachusetts men who dressed up as Indians and threw a large quantity of tea into Boston Harbor. They protested a tax that Britain had imposed on the sale of tea. The tea belonged to a British concern, and its destruction didn't sit well with Parliament, which in early 1774 voted to close the port of Boston until Bostonians reimbursed the East India Company for three hundred and forty-two chests of its lost tea. Parliament also demanded restitution of the tax revenues that Royal customs officers would have collected had the tea not been destroyed.

Developments occurred swiftly after that. Defiant Bostonians balked at making the payments. In May, General Thomas Gage arrived in Boston from England and became military governor of Massachusetts. He carried orders to close the port and to enforce other punitive measures ordered by London. In June 1774, British warships began a blockade of the port.

Born in Boston in 1706, Benjamin Franklin had moved to Philadelphia as a teenager. He had long been a significant influence on Pennsylvania politics, and in 1764, the Pennsylvania Assembly sent him to London as its agent. By 1774, Franklin had become the agent for several other colonies as well. As the rift widened between the North American colonies and the British government in London, Franklin did what he could diplomatically to resolve the conflicts.

Benjamin Franklin

Although Franklin's critics in Britain accused him of promoting the troubles, Dr. Joseph Priestley, a friend who saw him frequently in London during this time, remarked in his memoirs, "I can bear witness that he was so far from promoting (American independence), as was generally supposed, that he took every method in his power to prevent a rupture between the two countries."

Although Priestley and Franklin shared strong interests in electricity and the natural sciences, "the difference with America breaking out at this time, our conversation was chiefly of a political nature," Priestley wrote. "He urged so much the doctrine of forbearance, that for some time he was unpopular with the Americans on that account, as too much a friend to Great Britain."

By early 1775, Franklin had decided to return to Pennsylvania. "The last day that he spent in England, . . . we passed together, without any other company; and much of the time was employed in reading American newspapers, especially accounts of the reception which the Boston port bill met with in America; and as he read the addresses to the inhabitants of Boston... the tears trickled down his cheeks," Priestley said.

Franklin left London on March 20, a Monday, a passenger aboard the *Captain Osborne*, a Pennsylvania packet ship bound for Philadelphia. "I had a passage of

Joseph Priestley

six weeks, the weather constantly so moderate that a London wherry (rowboat) might have accompanied us all the way," Franklin wrote to Priestley.

The news that Benjamin Franklin had returned to Philadelphia after an absence of nearly nine years electrified the city. As a visitor from Massachusetts, Samuel Curwen, wrote in his journal for Sunday, May 7: "Dr. Franklin arrived last night, which was announced by ringing of bells, to the great joy of the city. I cannot but promise myself some good, as his knowledge and experience must have influence in the approaching Congress, which will, I doubt not, listen to his judgment."

Back in England, Joseph Priestley nourished his memories of his many conversations with Franklin during the winter of 1774–1775, which both men had spent in London. "My winter's residence in London was the means of improving my acquaintance with Dr. Franklin," Priestley wrote. "I was seldom many days without seeing him."

In his memoirs, Priestley described these conversations with Franklin: "He dreaded the war, and often said that if the difference should come to an open rupture, it would be a war of ten years, and he should not live to see the end of it. In reality the war lasted near eight years, but he did live to see the happy termination of it. That the issue would be favorable to America, he never doubted. The English, he used to say, may take all our great towns, but that will not give them possession of the country."

Writing to Priestley on Tuesday, May 16, 1775, Franklin reported that the Pennsylvania Assembly had lost little time in selecting him to represent the colony in the Second Continental Congress. It convened in Philadelphia on Wednesday, May 10, only four days after Franklin's return. "I got home in the evening, and the next morning was unanimously chosen by the Assembly a delegate to the Congress, now sitting," Franklin wrote.

In May 1775, Samuel Curwen, a Loyalist merchant from Salem, Massachusetts, had come to Philadelphia aboard a schooner, the HMS Lively, that was ultimately destined for the English port of Dover. Before crossing the Atlantic, the schooner made a nine-day stop at Philadelphia, and Curwen, who was fifty-nine, took advantage of the hiatus to determine whether Pennsylvania might be a place for him to live

Samuel Curwen

until the Revolutionary winds buffeting Massachusetts subsided. As he left The Lively, he was "hoping to find an asylum amongst Quakers and Dutchmen, who, I presume, from former experience, have too great a regard for ease and property to sacrifice either at this time of doubtful disputation."

Curwen had decided to leave Salem soon after the fighting at Lexington and Concord on April 19. Encouraged by the drubbing that colonial militia gave British regulars, the people of Massachusetts quickly let "their tempers to get more and more soured and malevolent against all moderate men, whom they see fit to reproach as enemies of their country by the name of Tories, among whom I am unhappily (although unjustly) ranked," the Loyalist wrote in his journal entry for Thursday, May 4, the day he disembarked at Philadelphia. Rather than remain in Massachusetts, Curwen thought it would be safer to go into self-imposed exile, either in Pennsylvania or in Britain.

His experiences in Philadelphia quickly dashed any hopes of staying in Pennsylvania. For instance, he had notified his kinsman, a Philadelphian named Samuel Smith, of his arrival, and Smith came down to the wharf and met Curwen as he was leaving The Lively. "He was pleased to come on board . . . and his first salutation, 'We will protect you, though a Tory,' embarrassed me not a little," the traveler wrote in his journal.

Nonetheless, Curwen and Smith quickly "fell into a friendly conversation," and Smith took him to his residence for dinner. The visit was cordial enough, and Smith invited Curwen "to make his house my home during my stay here," but Curwen declined. "I took leave, and went in pursuit of lodgings, and on enquiring at several houses, ascertained they were full, or for particular reasons would not take me; and so many refused as made it fearful whether, like Cain, I had not a discouraging mark upon me, or a strong feature of Toryism," he wrote.

Not everyone rebuffed him. Curwen said that he "at length arrived at one Mrs. Swords, a widow lady, in Chestnut Street, with whom I found quarters."

The next day—Friday, May 5, 1775—Curwen was disturbed to "find the drums beating, colors flying, and detachments of newly raised militia parading the streets."

The spectacle was so alarming that the traveler concluded, the "whole country appears determined to assume a military character, and this city, throwing off her pacific

Bells rang throughout Philadelphia to announce and celebrate Benjamin Franklin's return from London in May 1775.

aspect, is forming military companies, a plan being laid for thirty-three. Composed of all ranks and nations, uniting shoulder to shoulder, they form so many patriotic bands to oppose . . . the progress and increase of Parliamentary authority."

Even the pacifistic Quakers, "not to be behind in manifesting their aversion, have obtained permission of the city committee to make up two companies of Friends, exclusively, and they are to be commanded by Samuel Marshall and Thomas Mifflin, both of that persuasion."

Curwen was surprised when an acquaintance from Massachusetts, "Joseph Lee, hearing I was in the city, came to see me, and advised my going to London."

By Saturday, May 6, Curwen was sufficiently discouraged by his Philadelphia experiences that he abandoned any thought of staying on in Pennsylvania. "I have . . . consulted the few friends I think it worth while to advise with, and, on the result, am determined to proceed to London in the vessel in which I came here," he wrote.

News of political events traveled ever so slowly, to the frustration of Philadelphians who had a ravenous appetite for it. The sighting of a ship—possibly a trading ship called The James—coming up the Delaware River on Sunday, May 7, created a stir. "At 2 o'clock, at the wharf, a large collection of people were waiting news from London, Captain Robinson having just anchored," Curwen reported. The vessel brought word that Parliament had passed the New England Restraining Act, which restricted merchants in Massachusetts and the other New England colonies—Connecticut, New Hampshire, and Rhode Island—to dealing only with British and West Indies merchants.

For a merchant visiting a distant city, Curwen had excellent connections. On the evening of Tuesday, May 9, he "passed the evening" at the home of a prominent and politically active Quaker, Joseph Reed. Other guests included "three of the Virginia delegates" to the Continental Congress—Richard Henry Lee, Colonel Benjamin Harrison, and Colonel George Washington.

"I stayed till 12 o'clock, the conversation being chiefly on the most feasible and prudent method of stopping up the channel of the Delaware, to prevent the coming up of any large ships to the city," Curwen reported.

"Early in the morning" of Wednesday, May 10, news swept the city that congressional delegates from New York and New England were approaching Philadelphia, Curwen reported. To greet them, "a great number of persons rode out several miles," he added.

"About 11 o'clock, the cavalcade appeared . . .; first, two hundred or three hundred gentlemen on horseback, preceded . . . by the newly-chosen city military officers, two and two, with drawn swords, followed by John Hancock and Samuel Adams, in a (four-wheeled carriage called a) phaeton and pair, the former looking as if his journey and high living, or solicitude to support the dignity of the first man in Massachusetts, had impaired his health.

"Next came John Adams and Thomas Gushing in a single-horse chaise; behind followed Robert Treat Paine, and after him the New York delegation, and some from the Province of Connecticut," Curwen wrote in his journal.

On Thursday, May 11, the Massachusetts merchant had tea with his friend from New England, Joseph Lee, and "Mr. Lee again repeated his advice of my going to London."

On Friday, May 12, Curwen reported that he sent his baggage on board The Lively; took leave of Lee and other friends, and "I went on board The Lively."

Curwen was traveling alone. His wife of twenty-five years, Abigail Russell Curwen, had refused to accompany him. He had attempted to persuade her, but she remained in Salem, "her apprehensions of danger from an incensed soldiery, a people licentious and enthusiastically mad and broken loose from all the restraints of law or religion being less terrible to her than a short passage on the ocean."

Four days later, as The Lively descended the Delaware, the ship encountered a Philadelphia-bound schooner from Nantucket, whose captain "brought me a letter from Nathan Goodale," a Massachusetts friend who had moved offshore to Nantucket to ride out the political storm. Curwen had enough time to dash off a few lines for Goodale, most of them about his visit to Philadelphia. He emphasized that he had concluded that Pennsylvania wouldn't serve as a haven for Massachusetts Loyalists. "The inhabitants are displeased that the New Englanders make it their city of refuge," he said. He added, "Mr. Joseph Lee leads a recluse life there."

Curwen gave the letter to the captain with a request that he forward it to Goodale when he returned to Nantucket.

At sea on Thursday, June 1, a sloop-of-war from Boston, The Otter, "brought us to at 9 o'clock, and informed us all was quiet when she left." Officers aboard The Otter informed the captain of The Lively that forty-five British troop transport ships, along with three generals, had arrived at Boston in late May. The rebellious colonials had amassed a force of fifteen thousand men and awaited direction from the Continental Congress. Also, "a great fire . . . beginning at the barrack stores on the docks" had destroyed a substantial part of Boston.

"She detained us two hours in order to send letters to England," Curwen wrote.

His ship arrived at Dover, England, on Monday, July 3, ending a voyage of seven weeks.

Nine years passed before Samuel Curwen returned to Massachusetts, then a part of the United States, in 1784.

July 1776

Disarming Tories

Subtle changes occurred in the official records kept by the Pennsylvania Council of Safety in the weeks after the Continental Congress declared independence from Great Britain in July 1776. By early August, the words "colony" and "colonies" virtually disappeared from the record.

As late as April 1776, minutes of the council's meetings referred to "the Province of Pennsylvania" and described England's rebellious colonies as "the united American colonies." They also referred to the American Revolutionary War as "the dispute between Great Britain and these colonies."

A definite shift in nomenclature took place between July 4, the date on which the Declaration of Independence was approved, and the Council of Safety's August 5 session. The records now referred to "the state of Pennsylvania." The phrase "the united American colonies" gave way to "the American states" and to "the states of America." By year-end, the council had begun to receive correspondence referring to the "United States of America."

In September 1776, Pennsylvania adopted a constitution that called for the creation of a new government to replace the one used by the proprietary Penn family. Organized in

March 1777, the Pennsylvania Supreme Executive Council and the state's General Assembly "by joint ballot" elected Thomas Wharton, Jr., as president. Over the next several months, the council established county and municipal governments and appointed officials to run them. On June 10, for example, it appointed justices of the peace in York and Northumberland counties.

Thomas Wharton Jr., President, the Pennsylvania Supreme Executive Council

One of the newly appointed justices in Northumberland County was Colonel Samuel Hunter, who was also the commander of the Northumberland County Militia. By late 1777, Hunter, who was headquartered at Fort Augusta in Sunbury, needed to resolve a dilemma.

On one hand, Hunter had been ordered to confiscate the firearms of Northumberland County men who hadn't sworn allegiance to Pennsylvania's new government. On the other hand, he recognized the need of the county's homesteaders—regardless of their political beliefs—to defend themselves against Indian war parties sent out by the British military to raid the frontier settlements. In selecting homesteads to attack, the warriors weren't distinguishing between pioneer families that supported the Revolution and those that remained loyal to King George III.

So, Hunter procrastinated. "I received orders from your excellency to disarm all persons in this county that refuses to take the oath of allegiance," Hunter said in an October 27, letter to President Wharton of the Supreme Executive Council. ". . . At that time I could not with any propriety take the arms from several on the frontiers that was willing to stand in their own defense against the savages, yet never said they would not take the oath, but wanted time to consider of it."

But the time for consideration has passed "and a number not willing to take said oath, your orders will Immediately be put in execution," Hunter said.

As this suggests, Pennsylvanians remained sharply divided politically more than a year after the Congress declared independence from England. Although many supported the Declaration of Independence, many others believed that it wasn't too late for Britain and the states to resolve their differences peacefully. Many of these people continued to feel a strong loyalty to King George.

Thus, Pennsylvania found itself split into two camps—the liberal Whigs who supported Independence, the Continental Congress, and the new state and local governments—and the conservative Loyalists, or Tories, who opposed independence from Britain and didn't want to war against the king's armies.

There was also a third group. It consisted of people who feared that were the British to win, they would find themselves and their families in jeopardy for having pledged allegiance to Pennsylvania and the United States. After all, would the British look favorably on men who had formally sided with the rebels?

In June 1777, as the divide widened, the Pennsylvania General Assembly passed legislation requiring "all male white inhabitants of this state, (except of the counties of Bedford, Northumberland, and Westmoreland) above the age of eighteen years" to swear their allegiance to Pennsylvania and the United States. In the minutes of the state's Supreme Executive Council, this is sometimes described as the "Oath of Allegiance" and sometimes as the "Test of Allegiance."

Whigs eagerly sought out the justices of the peace to administer the oath, Loyalists did their best to ignore the new law, and fence-sitters found themselves in dire straits. As one man explained to a Northampton County magistrate in 1777, "It is so uncertain upon what side God Almighty will bestow the victory."

The act spelled out specific consequences for Pennsylvanians who, in the parlance of the Executive Council, "have not manifested their attachment to the American cause." To begin with, these men could no longer own firearms and "shall be disarmed" by officers of the state militia. Furthermore, they would become "incapable of holding any office or place of trust in this state; serving on juries; suing for any debts; electing or being elected; (and) buying, selling or transferring any lands, tenements or hereditaments . . ."

The tensions between factions had been growing since the early 1770s when the colonies had begun organizing militias. Pennsylvania was no exception. As early as January 1775, the Committee of Safety of Bucks County voted to formally and "earnestly recommend to the people of this county to form themselves into associations, in their respective townships, to improve themselves in the military art, that they may be rendered capable of affording their

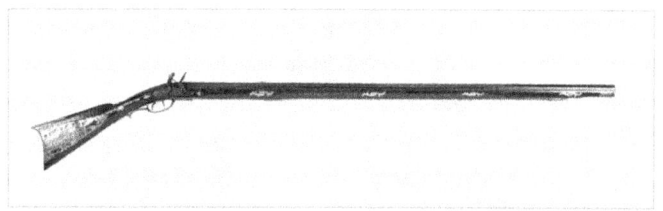

A Pennsylvania/Kentucky rifle. Photo courtesy of John Spitzer.

country that aid which its particular necessities may at any time require."

The men who turned out to join these military associations soon came to be called Associators. Those who declined to participate became known as Non-Associators.

As the war shifted from Boston to New York in 1776, Pennsylvania's Whig government began to confiscate the weapons of Non-Associators. This action didn't sit well with Loyalists, who regarded themselves as good citizens. Some even had the gumption to refuse to give up their guns when militiamen came to their houses with orders to collect them.

For instance, the Bucks County Committee of Safety learned that "sundry persons had refused to surrender the arms in their possession to the collectors of arms," members of the militia who had been appointed to confiscate the weapons of Non-Associators who lived in their districts. In a July 1 resolve, the committee decided that when "such refusal shall happen in any township," an officer of the county militia would select "such number of men as he shall apprehend proper and sufficient to enforce" the order.

In mid-December 1776, with British and Hessian soldiers posted along the Delaware River—some as close as twenty miles from Philadelphia—and the Continental

Army camped in Bucks County along the river's west shore, the state Council of Safety asked "General Washington to issue orders immediately for the militia of Bucks and Northampton counties forthwith to join his army, and to send out parties to disarm every person who does not obey the summons." The council also recommended that the militiamen should "seize and treat as enemies all such as shall attempt to oppose the execution of this measure."

Weapons taken from Tories were frequently given to Pennsylvania soldiers for use in fighting the British. In Cumberland County, for example, "arms taken from Non-Associators in Antrim and Peters Townships" in late 1776 were relayed to Colonel John Allison, commander of Pennsylvania troops preparing to leave for New Jersey, "and put into the hands of his battalion, then under marching orders for Amboy." Amboy, known today as Perth Amboy, was across the Arthur Kill from British-held Staten Island in New York.

Writing at Fort Augusta on December 24, 1776, Colonel Samuel Hunter reported that "a company of volunteers marched off this day out of my battalion of Associators to join General Washington" along the Delaware. The men leaving Sunbury "are all armed and accoutered in the best manner I could, and they have chose(n) for their captain Major John Lee."

As the volunteers prepared for the hundred-mile march over the mountains, Hunter realized that a number lacked firearms. To obtain weapons for these men, Hunter confiscated guns, apparently from Non-Associators, with a promise that the state would compensate them.

"I have impressed several guns, blankets, and other necessaries for the men, and has had them appraised, which Captain Lee will give you a list of," Hunter reported.

Records in the Pennsylvania Archives from 1776 and 1777 show that men whose guns were seized generally received compensation from the state. For example, on January 8, 1777, the Pennsylvania Council of Safety authorized payments totaling £109 for the weapons seized in Peters and Antrim townships, which today are part of Franklin County.

In another instance, on January 29, 1777, the Pennsylvania Council of Safety authorized payment of £42, for arms taken and appraised in Bedford County from Non-Associators in the District of the 1st Battalion."

During the summer of 1777, British troop movements prompted Pennsylvania authorities to greater urgency in confiscating firearms from men who hadn't taken loyalty oaths. In July, thousands of British and Hessians soldiers began boarding transport ships in New York Harbor. The Americans quickly realized that Major General William Howe planned a movement of some type, but no one knew his destination. In Philadelphia, President Wharton suspected that Howe had become "intent on invading this state."

"A fleet of two hundred forty sail of ships of war and transports actually sailed from the Bay of New York, with a fair wind on Tuesday last," Wharton reported on July 28. "On Friday, a very great part of this fleet were seen on the coast of New Jersey, within eight or ten leagues of the Bay of Delaware, striving to gain an entrance against a head wind."

Instead, the British sailed into the Chesapeake Bay and landed in late August at Elkton, Maryland, about sixty miles southwest of Philadelphia.

For Pennsylvania's Whigs, the time had come to force the Tories to give up their guns. On August 27, the Supreme Executive Committee ordered the Philadelphia militia to conduct a house-to-house search of all "inhabitants of the City of Philadelphia who have not manifested their attachment to the American cause for firearms, swords, and bayonets." The owners of the confiscated weapons would "be paid for them at an appraised value," the committee said. The weapons themselves would be "delivered to such of the militia . . . who are at present unarmed and have been called into the field."

In late summer, as southeastern Pennsylvania braced for a British invasion, the Supreme Executive Committee called out the militia. At Fort Augusta, Colonel Hunter responded that he intended for the militia troops "of this county to march out immediately."

Meanwhile, he reported that outlying settlers had recently observed signs of pro-British warriors in the upper Susquehanna River Valley and had become "afraid of the Indians coming down upon our frontiers."

Hunter added, "We are badly off in this county for want of arms and ammunition." A shipment of "five hundred stand of arms . . . will be very much wanted in case we are invaded here by ye savages."

Hunter's letter was dated September 10, the day before the Battle of Brandywine, when the Continental Army attempted to stop the British army from advancing on Philadelphia. Pennsylvania militia troops—some no doubt using confiscated firearms—fought alongside Continental troops at Brandywine Creek. Pennsylvania militiamen

Colonel Samuel Hunter of the Northumberland County Militia lived in Fort Augusta at Sunbury. When militia troops marched off to join General Washington on the Delaware River in December 1776, Hunter confiscated firearms from Loyalists in his region, then reissued the weapons to the departing soldiers. Photo shows officers quarters inside the Fort Augusta model on the grounds of the Northumberland County Historical Society, Sunbury.

again joined Continental regulars in attacking the British at Germantown on October 4.

Both actions resulted in defeats for the Americans.

As winter approached, the British army occupied Philadelphia. From exile in Lancaster, the Council of Safety on November 8 ordered officials in nine counties—Berks, Bucks, Chester, Cumberland, Lancaster, Northampton, Northumberland, Philadelphia, and York—"to collect without delay from such of the inhabitants of the said respective counties as have not taken the Oath of Allegiance . . . or who have aided or assisted the enemy, arms and accouterments, blankets, woolen and linsey-woolsey cloth, linen, shoes, and stockings, for the army."

Linsey-woolsey was a fabric made of both wool and linen.

Within six weeks, Washington took the Continental Army to Valley Forge, about twenty-five miles northwest of Philadelphia, for a winter of deprivation. Blankets, shoes, and stockings confiscated from the Loyalists proved a boon for many a rebel soldier.

Summer 1777

Second-guessing General Howe

As the summer of 1777 began, George Washington took a special interest in monitoring British troop movements in and about New York from Camp Middle Brook in New Jersey's Watchung Mountains.

The camp was about thirty-five miles southwest of Manhattan, close enough for Washington's spies, British deserters, and American observers to keep the commander-in-chief apprised of the movements of Major General William Howe's army in New York and eastern New Jersey.

Military intelligence also informed Washington that a second British army, led by General John Burgoyne, had started to march south from Canada, venturing into the region of Lakes George and Champlain in upstate New York. The lakes lay between Albany and Montreal, with American-held Fort Ticonderoga defending a strategic portage between the lakes against any British move toward Albany.

Washington kept his focus on the British presence in and around Manhattan.

"A deserter from the 37th (British Regiment) this morning says that yesterday orders were given for his regiment and ten more to hold themselves in readiness to embark from (Perth) Amboy. And that the inhabitants of

George Washington

Amboy, Brunswick, etcetera, capable of bearing arms were ordered to garrison New York," the general reported in a June 7 letter to Major General John Sullivan.

Washington added, "An intelligent person who left New York (on) the 5th says many vessels were fitted up for horses and that . . . the transports were prepared for troops and that some that were to go on board had come over from Staten Island. If so, the fleet is near sailing."

A year earlier, General Howe, the commanding general of all British forces in North America, had occupied Staten Island, and then in a series of battles, had forced the Continentals to leave Long Island, Brooklyn, and Manhattan. As Washington retreated to eastern Pennsylvania in December 1776, Howe had posted English and Hessian soldiers at various places across New Jersey. Many of these soldiers

Major General William Howe

remained in place, especially in East Jersey, even after the American victories at Trenton on December 26, 1776, and January 2, 1777, and at Princeton on January 3, 1777.

After the Battle of Princeton, Washington took his army to Morristown, in northern New Jersey, for the winter. But in early summer: the British quietly and slowly began to withdraw from New Jersey. On June 29, for instance, a force of twelve hundred Continental soldiers under General Sullivan was near Metuchen, in central New Jersey, when "we heard the enemy's drums beat to arms, and we formed in line of battle," Lieutenant James McMichael noted in his journal.

To McMichael's surprise, instead of attacking, the English were returning to Perth Amboy, a New Jersey town about seven miles to the east on the Raritan Bay.

Four days later, Sullivan's men received "intelligence that the enemy had evacuated Amboy and gone to Staten Island," a short distance across Arthur Kill, a tidal strait that separated New Jersey and Staten Island.

Major General John Sullivan

A few days after that, Washington learned that Howe was preparing his troops for a voyage. American intelligence sources informed him on July 7 "that small craft are constantly plying between New York and the (British) fleet laden with officers, baggage, and stores put in packages and marked with their names and regiments, and that transports are fitted up with stalls over their main decks for the reception of horses."

Washington didn't know—and couldn't find out from his spies—what Howe was planning to do.

Then in early July, events two hundred and fifty miles away in upstate New York complicated the situation immensely. As General Burgoyne approached with a much larger force of British and Hessian troops, Continental troops withdrew from Fort Ticonderoga. Their withdrawal cleared the way for Burgoyne to bring his army farther south without much opposition, a possibility that gave Washington much concern.

Was Howe preparing to ship his troops high up the Hudson River and connect with Burgoyne? Writing on July 10 to John Hancock, the president of the Continental Congress sitting at Philadelphia, Washington noted: "The strong probability... is that General Howe will push against the Highland passes (along the Hudson River) to co-operate with General Burgoyne." With Howe's troops already aboard the transport ships, "a favorable wind and tide will carry him up in a few hours," Washington said.

Anticipating this possibility, Washington had already left Camp Middle Brook and moved his army twenty miles north to Morristown. "I shall, by the advice of my officers, move the army from hence tomorrow morning, towards the North (Hudson) River. If such should be his intention, we shall not be too early."

It was also possible that Howe had something else in mind. "On the other hand, if Philadelphia is his object, he can't get round (New Jersey) before we can arrive there, nor can he well debark his troops... and proceed across the land before we can oppose him," he told Hancock.

Whatever Howe did—and whenever he did it—Washington realized that his Continentals needed to be ready to react quickly.

Washington soon had the Continentals marching farther north. From Morristown, they marched the twenty miles north to Pompton Plains. Heavy rains had left the dirt roads "extremely deep and miry," Washington said. By July 15, the army had reached present-day Orange County, New York, stopping about eighteen miles from the west side of the Hudson, which Washington invariably referred to by its old name—the North River.

Along the way, his sources informed him that on July 13, some seventy British ships had left New York Harbor and sailed down to Sandy Hook along the New Jersey coast, "but whether they have since gone out to sea, I have not heard," Washington said in a July 16 letter to Hancock.

He wanted Hancock to know that until he could determine "General Howe's real intentions, I have concluded to halt the army at this place, from whence I can march either forward or return, as circumstances may require."

If Howe intended to reverse course suddenly and sail up the Hudson, Washington wanted strong forces on each side of the Hudson. To accomplish this, on the 16th, he ordered General Sullivan to take his men across to the Hudson's east shore "as soon as possible" if he hadn't already done so.

On July 24, "when, receiving certain information that the fleet had actually sailed from Sandy Hook . . . and the concurring sentiment of everyone, (though I acknowledge my doubts of it were strong,) that Philadelphia was the object, we counter-marched, and got to Coryell's Ferry on the Delaware . . . on the 27th," Washington wrote in an August 5 letter to his brother, John Augustine Washington.

The ferry crossed the Delaware between the present-day towns of Lambertville, New Jersey, and New Hope, Pennsylvania.

The general, who camped at Coryell's Ferry himself for several days in late July, regarded the ferry, which was about thirty-eight miles northeast of Philadelphia, as both strategic and convenient for moving troops across the Delaware. On July 31, he advised General Sullivan that, when Sullivan's division came south toward Philadelphia, "the route

Coryell's Ferry once crossed the Delaware River at this point between Lambertville, New Jersey, and New Hope, Pennsylvania. In this view, New Hope is on the far shore. General Washington ordered the Continental Army to cross here as the soldiers marched south from New York State to oppose British troops movements in southeastern Pennsylvania. The two armies fought at the Battle of the Brandywine in September 1777.

by Coryell's will be best, as there is a sufficient number of boats to transport the troops and baggage in a very short time." The same day he instructed Major General Israel Putnam "to order the two brigades . . . to march immediately towards Philadelphia through Morristown and over Coryell's Ferry, where boats will be ready for them."

The American commander told his brother that he was highly displeased that his soldiers had had to travel such long distances in sultry summer weather. "Since General Howe's remove from the Jerseys, the troops under my command have been more harassed by marching, and counter-marching, than by anything that has happened to them in the course of the campaign," he said

After leaving their camp near the Hudson on July 24, the Continentals had marched more than a hundred miles to reach the Delaware four days later. Washington said that he deplored "the fatigue . . . and injury, which men must sustain by long marches in such extreme heat as we have felt for the last five days."

Back in New York, General Sullivan had taken his division across the Hudson by August 3 and camped on the river's east side. Washington instructed him: "If you receive intelligence which you can certainly depend upon that the enemy's fleet . . . are upon the coast of New England, you are then to move on to Peeks Kill, without waiting any orders from me." Along the Hudson, Peekskill was about forty miles north of Manhattan.

On August 4, Washington finally received news of Howe. "On Thursday and Friday last their fleet, consisting of two hundred and twenty-eight sail, were beating off the Capes of Delaware, as if they intended to come in," he wrote. Just as it was beginning to look as if Howe planned a move against Philadelphia, "they have stood out to sea again, but how far, or where they are going, remains to be known," the general wrote.

A few days later, an express rider reached Washington with word that "a large fleet of ships, consisting of upwards of two hundred sail was seen off" the coast of southern Delaware, near Maryland's Eastern Shore. It was sailing to the southeast. That was on August 7.

On August 7, 1777 an express rider reached General Washington in Neshaminy, Pennsylvania, with news that a large fleet of British ships had been seen in the Atlantic Ocean sailing to the southeast past southern Delaware.

"They were seen again upon the 8th, nearly in the same situation," the general told Sullivan in an August 14 letter. On August 20, he informed Major General Horatio Gates, "I am now of opinion that Charles Town (South Carolina) is the present object of General Howe's attention."

On August 15, Howe's fleet was sighted off Virginia, a development that raised the possibility his ships might sail into the Chesapeake Bay. On August 22, Washington wrote that he had just learned—"by an express this minute come to hand from Congress"—that the British ships had "arrived in Chesapeake Bay, and are high up in the northeast part of it."

As it turned out, Howe took his army ashore at modern-day Elkton, Maryland, situated at the top of an arm of the bay, a location that let the British land about sixty miles southwest of Philadelphia. It was now clear that the British commander intended to march on Philadelphia, where the U.S. Congress was in session.

Washington realized that he needed to regroup quickly. On August 22, he summoned General Sullivan, by then in northern New Jersey, commanding a division of mostly Maryland troops as well as New Jersey militiamen. "You will immediately march with your division and join this army, proceeding with all convenient expedition, but not in such a manner as to injure the troops. You will cross the Delaware at Coryell's Ferry and avoid Philadelphia in your march down," Washington wrote.

Three weeks later and about thirty miles southwest of Philadelphia, Washington attempted to stop Howe's advance at the village of Chadds Ford along Brandywine Creek. The Battle of Brandywine Creek was fought on September 11, 1777.

The British outmaneuvered the Americans, who retreated. The result cleared the way for the British to enter Philadelphia, which they did on September 26. Their approach prompted members of Congress to flee a hundred miles west to York, Pennsylvania.

January 1782

Robbing the rebels

One moonlight night in late January 1782, a Bucks County man, James Snodgrass, took his wife for a ride across the snow-covered countryside in his two-horse sleigh.

Snodgrass was the municipal collector of fines and taxes for the Township of New Britain. Ordinarily, he kept his collections at home, but a recent robbery in nearby Newtown had prompted Snodgrass to take precautions. When he and his wife left on the sleigh ride, he took "the public money with him rather than risk it at home in his absence," according to Joseph Hart, the county treasurer.

The man's concern was well justified. "Four armed men, about 9 o'clock in the evening, all on horseback, came to the house," Hart said in a report to President William Moore.

Chagrined that Snodgrass wasn't at home, the robbers demanded money. They forced his daughter, "a young girl scarce grown up, ... to get the keys, and, after much search, got nine Spanish dollars and a small sum of state money only," said Hart, who as Colonel Joseph Hart was also the commanding officer of the Bucks County Militia.

Angered that they had found so little money, the robbers decided that as a consolation, they would steal

Snodgrass's two young mares, but this didn't happen because these were the horses pulling the sleigh.

Evidence obtained much later proved that the Snodgrass robbery had been committed by the Doan Gang, which took its name from its leader, Moses Doan. He and his brothers lived in Plumstead Township in central Bucks County. "Their place of rendezvous was in a wild, secluded spot on the south bank of the Tohickon Creek, two miles above Point Pleasant," according to William Davis, the 19th century Bucks County historian.

Point Pleasant is a village along the Delaware River north of New Hope.

Greed motivated the men to commit the robberies. The perpetrators kept the money they stole. After each heist, they met to split the loot among the members of the gang and their accomplices. Even so, the historical record suggests that these men may have regarded themselves not as robbers but as Loyalist guerillas conducting a rear-guard action at a time when the British were losing the Revolutionary War.

By early 1782, the British and American armies were doing most of the fighting in Virginia and other southern states. Nonetheless, Pennsylvania continued to maintain its militia. It used the revenue brought in by the township tax collectors to finance militia operations. Members of a militia company were required to participate in drills. A militiaman who skipped a session was obligated to pay a fine to the tax collector in the township where his company was based. As Joseph Reed of the Supreme Executive Committee explained to Colonel Robert Levers of the Northampton County Militia in June 1781, "The serving militia are to be paid out of the fines of the delinquents . . ."

Legend has it that the Doan Gang had a hideout in the woods along Tohickon Creek, seen here just before it flows into the Delaware River at Point Pleasant.

The Bucks County robberies, which took place over several months, each one at the residence of a municipal collector of taxes and fines, hampered the county's effort to pay its militiamen. This fact alone gave the robberies political significance.

Consider the robbery that occurred on the night of Saturday, February 16, when two gang members invaded the residence of John Keith, the Upper Makefield Township collector of fines and taxes. Keith wasn't at home, and the robbers failed to find any money. One man decided he would steal "a gun, a sword, and bayonet which he found in the house . . . (but) the man who stood sentry at the kitchen door bid him take nothing but what belonged to the Congress," according to Keith's sister Sarah.

The first of these robberies—there were nine altogether—took place several days after the American victory at Yorktown in mid-October 1781. After so much time, it's impossible to know if news of General Cornwallis's October 19 surrender had prompted the crime. Still, on the

Holster pistol

night of October 22, robbers invaded the home of Joseph Hart, the county treasurer who was also the of the militia commander.

Hart, who lived in a stone house in Newtown, was at home, and the robbers, who carried flintlock pistols, came looking for money. They detained Hart at gunpoint and ransacked the residence by candlelight. After a thorough search, they forced Hart to give them the key to the nearby treasury building, where they found a combination of gold, silver, and paper money. Hart said later that their haul included packages of paper currency they had found under Hart's bed. According to Henry C. Mercer, the Bucks County historian, the stolen silver was valued at more than £735.

Hart said later that the robbers had kept him "under guard, as I think, upward of three hours. They left my house, but in so cautious a manner that I could not know the time of their final departure, as some of them were heard loitering out of doors, on both sides of the house, a considerable time after they had gone out of it."

Hart said there were at least twelve robbers, all of whom got away.

These home invasions occurred almost regularly. Writing on Monday, March 3, Colonel Hart notified President Moore that on the night of Thursday, February 28, two armed intruders "came to the house of Captain Ralph Williamson, collector of fines for the Township of Wrightstown . . . One of them slipped in, and the other sat upon his horse at the door." It was after 7 o'clock. Williamson himself wasn't home, but his wife and children were. A search of the house turned up £22 in hard money. The man said, "they did not want to hurt her nor the children, but if her husband had been at home, they had something to say (to) him."

The robbers rode off, and Mrs. Williamson "immediately called home her husband, who was only gone over to a neighbor's house." The robbers had departed by then.

"The next morning," Hart reported, "their tracks were . . . followed for several miles, notwithstanding they had made many turnings, windings, and sometimes separated to elude the pursuit, but all to no purpose."

Later that same night, an apparent home invasion was foiled in a nearby village. As Hart reported, "one of the next neighbors to the collector of the Township of Warminster, thinking he heard something about his house, jumped up in his shirt and slipped out, when he saw three men standing at a small distance. Two kept their standing, but the third advanced a few paces, and asked if that was the way to Dilworth's."

The neighbor didn't reply. Instead, he asked the stranger for his name and what were the men were doing there. When they didn't answer, he produced his pistol. "The villains then took to their heels, and his gun missing fire twice, and he being naked and not in a condition to pursue far, they all got off," Hart said. ". . . While such atrocious villains remain amongst us, no man who can be supposed to have money is safe. For my own part, I do not think I am, as they can collect too great a force for any common man to withstand."

A detailed account of the mid-February robbery at the Keith house survives because the tax collector's sister, Sarah Keith, who was also Keith's housekeeper, gave a deposition to a justice of the peace several days later.

"About 8 o'clock in the evening, her brother's house was surrounded by a number of armed men, and one of them entering the kitchen enquired if the man of the house was at home." He wasn't, and when Sarah acknowledged that, yes, her brother was the township tax collector, the robber demanded money.

She and a boy who lived with the family insisted that they didn't know where Keith kept the money even after the robber pointed a pistol at the boy's chest, After ordering Sarah to accompany him with a lighted candle, the intruder began a room-to-room search of the residence.

In her brother's bedroom, the robber found a locked chest and directed Sarah to unlock it. She did so, but the man didn't find any money. "He searched . . . every other chest (of) drawers and cupboards that he found, and almost every part of the house," but failed to find any money.

It was this robber who wanted to but didn't steal John Keith's gun and sword. Eventually, "he . . . left them and went off with the others without taking anything but a few biscuit(s) he found in the kitchen," Sarah said.

Although Sarah couldn't identify the intruder, she was able to provide a detailed description.

"The one who came into the house appeared about five foot ten inches high, about twenty-two or twenty-three years old with black hair, dark complexion, (and a) smooth face," she said.

She also got a good look at his clothing. He wore "a large scalloped hat, a light grey . . . bearskin great coat with a large falling collar of the same." He kept the coat "buttoned up so that his other clothes could not be seen, except his pale blue yarn stockings and calf skin shoes with silver buckles of the French pattern."

In time, two young men—Jesse and Solomon Vickers—were arrested, charged with felony and burglary, jailed in Newtown, convicted, and sentenced for their parts in the robberies. The court ordered Jesse Vickers to be hanged in early August. As the date for his execution approached, Vickers said he would provide the authorities with detailed information about the robberies, and the Supreme Executive Council postponed his hanging until August 14.

Solomon Vickers quickly joined his brother in turning state's evidence. By August 9, the brothers had given up the names of nearly a score of robbers—Moses, Aaron, and Mahlon Doan chief among them; had identified nine Bucks County residents as accomplices or accessories; and disclosed details of nine robberies, including the October 1781 raid on the county treasury.

In the hours before the treasury raid, "Moses Doan rode through the town to see if the coast was clear," Jesse Vickers said. The robbery began as gang members surrounded Colonel Hart's house.

"I stood sentinel at the gate," Vickers said.

Others "went in and presented a pistol to Mr. Hart's breast and made him deliver up the money and key of the office."

When the robbers took the loot and left the treasury building, they rode to Wrightstown, a village along the Durham Road, about four miles to the northwest. The gang stopped at the Wrightstown schoolhouse to divide the money. "There was sixteen or seventeen full shares, which was near a hundred forty dollars hard, and about as much state money," Jesse Vickers said.

As the Vickers boys described it, preparing for the treasury raid had become something of a community project with several people lending assistance but not taking part. Not only had John Atkinson, a Newtown gunsmith,

Joseph Reed

repaired flintlock pistols used by the robbers, but he had also provided information used in planning the raid. Amos White, who lived in Buckingham, on "the Sunday before the robbery of (the) treasury (had) delivered flints to Mahlon Doan which he had purchased in Philadelphia for him." The gunflints were used on that expedition, Vickers said. Also, John Tomlinson, who lived near Newtown, had helped plan the raid and had provided material support and information.

Vickers said that he visited the Tomlinson place near Newtown a few days before the robbery. When he went into the barn, he "saw six or seven guns, and Moses and Aaron Doan cleaning the . . . guns and making cartridges and bullets." He added that he tagged along when the men went into Tomlinson's house for dinner.

He said that "Tomlinson and the two Doans pressed him to go with them to rob the treasury," but he refused because "it was dangerous, that there was a guard over the treasury. Tomlinson replied that he had a man in town that acquainted him with every thing that passed in Newtown."

In the end, it came out that at least one of the tax collectors, Ralph Williamson, was in cahoots with the robbers. In sworn statements that he made as the date for his hanging drew near, Jesse Vickers accused two Bucks County tax collectors, Williamson and Moses Winder, of helping to plan the crimes.

Vickers also alleged that Captain Williamson had helped plan the robbery of his own house. According to Vickers, Williamson and one of the leaders of the gang, John Tomlinson, "had agreed that when Williamson should collect about eighty pounds, John Tomlinson was to send two fellows to rob him, and Williamson was to be absent at the shoemaker's."

But this scheme fell through. "Colonel Hart came to Williamson's house the afternoon before he was to have been robbed," Vickers said, took the revenue from Williamson, and "hurried the money to the office."

Vickers added, "Williamson went to John Tomlinson and told him that old Hart, the damned rascal, had come and carried the money to the office." Williamson said he had another thirty pounds to collect and would let Tomlinson know when he had the revenue in hand.

Williamson kept his word, and "John Tomlinson sent Moses Doan and some other person who took the money from Williamson's wife. Williamson was at the shoemaker's," Vickers said. When the robbers divided the loot, "Williamson got the largest share," according to Vickers.

Vickers said that at one point, he and another member of the gang, Aaron Doan, went to the house of tax collector Moses Winder, who lived in Lower Makefield Township on a farm along the road between Newtown and the Yardley ferry on the Delaware.

"Winder told them he was sorry they had not come a little sooner for . . . Captain Stillwell, his neighbor, had just received a large sum of money (near £200) to pay the militia, and he might easily be robbed of it." Winder said that he knew Stilwell "had no arms in his house, for he had reconnoitered him for that purpose."

Documentation of a robbery at Stillwell's house couldn't be located.

When the treasury loot was split up, some of it went to Winder, Atkinson, and Joseph Tomlinson.

Around Thursday, March 28, 1782, Solomon Vickers and three of the Doans—Abram, Joseph, and Levi—broke into the house of a collector named Smith, who lived in a section of upper Bucks called "the swamp." They had been told by an accomplice—a man named Richardson, who kept a tavern in Quakertown—that this "was a proper time to attack Smith . . . as he had a quantity of money . . ."

The moon was nearly full on the night of the raid, and "we met in a piece of woods by the road, and then proceeded to Richardson's Tavern," Vickers said. "We halted there and drank about two dollars' worth." When they left to go to Smith's house, "Richardson's brother went with us and shew (sic) us the way."

It was nearly midnight when the brigands arrived and broke into the residence through a door to the kitchen. But Smith had already turned his collections over to Colonel

Built during the 1730s, the Half-Moon Inn was a well-known Newtown tavern during the American Revolutionary War. The Newtown Historic Association now operates it as a museum.

Hart and had little for the robbers to take. "We got from him one French crown, it being all the money we could find," Vickers said. "After he had shown us his receipt from the treasurer, we left the house."

Richardson was supposed to receive money for providing information to the gang, "but as we got but one French Crown, he got none," Vickers said.

The Doan Gang committed eight other robberies in the months following the October 1781 raid on the county treasury.

Jesse and Solomon Vickers received full pardons from the Supreme Executive Council of Pennsylvania on September 18, 1782.

One gang member, Moses Doan, was shot and killed in 1783 while surrendering to a militia officer, Colonel Robert Gibson.

Two others—Levi Doan and his cousin Abraham Doan—were hanged in Philadelphia in 1788. They were

This historical marker about the Doan Gang stands along Point Pleasant Pike about half a mile southwest of Gardenville.

buried at the Plumstead Friends Meetinghouse near Gardenville.

When the militia attempted to arrest Moses Winder, the Lower Makefield tax collector, at his residence, his brother Aaron hid him in the cellar. Winder eluded the authorities and, in 1783, moved to Canada, where he settled in the Province of New Brunswick.

More than a century later, in November 1884, a ninety-three-year-old Canadian man, Levi Doan, received two visitors at his house in Humberstone, "a little town in Welland County, not far west of Niagara Falls" in the Province of Ontario. The visitors—a Mr. Reid and a Mr. Pratt—interviewed the elderly man about his father, the late Aaron Doan, and jotted down his answers. He told them that his father's five brothers were Moses, Levi, Thomas, Joseph, and Mahlon Doan; and his three sisters, Hetty, Polly, and Betsey.

The grave of Levi Doan, hanged in Philadelphia in 1788 for his part in the robberies, is located just outside of the cemetery at the Plumstead Friends Meeting near Gardenville. His tombstone notes that he was "an outlaw."

Of the six brothers, only Thomas, a child during the Revolution, wasn't ever implicated as a gang member.

When the war ended, Levi Doan reported, "Aaron, Thomas, Joseph, and the three sisters came to Canada."

"What became of your Uncle Mahlon Doan?" the visitors asked.

Although Mahlon Doan had been captured and imprisoned by the Pennsylvania authorities, as the war ended, "he escaped from prison and went on board a ship at New York on which were four hundred Loyalists," Levi Doan said. "I believe they sailed for England. We never heard any more of Mahlon."

Following the visit, Mr. Reid sent a report to a Doan family researcher, Alfred J. Doan, of Jersey City, New Jersey, who had arranged for Reid and Pratt to visit the elderly man.

In January 1885, historian Henry C. Mercer read part of Reid's report at a meeting of the Bucks County Historical Society.

May 1781
From York to Yorktown

In many ways, the American Revolution was a young man's war. The commander-in-chief, George Washington, was 49.

Gilbert du Motier, known better as the Marquis de Lafayette, was nineteen when he purchased a French ship, arranged for the transport of military supplies and several French officers, and set sail for America in April 1777. In July 1777, Congress commissioned him a major general. He served without pay. Washington met Lafayette in August at a dinner in Philadelphia.

By age twenty-three, Lafayette had proved himself in battle and was leading an army against the British in Virginia. Lafayette was twenty-four when he faced General Cornwallis at Yorktown along the York River in southeastern Virginia.

Brigadier General Anthony Wayne, born in Chester County in southeast Pennsylvania, was twenty when Benjamin Franklin employed him as a surveyor and sent him to Nova Scotia. He was thirty when he organized a militia company in 1775, and thirty-one when he became colonel of the 4th Pennsylvania battalion in 1776. A year later,

Gilbert du Motier, the Marquis de Lafayette

he was appointed brigadier general. Wayne was thirty-six when he led the Pennsylvania Line to Yorktown.

On January 1, 1781—coincidentally, Wayne's thirty-sixth birthday—the rank-and-file Pennsylvania soldiers in winter camp at Morristown, New Jersey, mutinied. The men hadn't been paid in months, and the three-year enlistment terms of many soldiers had expired long ago, but no one had discharged them.

Without permission and in defiance of their officers, the Pennsylvanians marched out of camp in a body, headed

General Anthony Wayne

for Philadelphia where they intended to demand their overdue payments.

Wayne met the soldiers in Princeton, New Jersey—less than thirty-five miles from British-held New York. Sensing an opportunity, Sir Henry Clinton, the British commander at Manhattan, sent two agents to Princeton to encourage the mutineers to defect.

The British eagerly received news of the mutiny, an American spy reported to Lieutenant Colonel Jacob Crane at Elizabeth, New Jersey. "Nothing could possibly have given them so much pleasure," Crane said in relaying the information to Wayne. ". . . They expect those in mutiny will immediately join them."

Wayne soon learned from another source that the British had a dozen flat-bottomed boats across from Staten Island at Perth Amboy, ready to take the mutineers across New York Harbor over to the British lines in New York.

In a January 8 letter to Washington, Wayne reported that he was negotiating with a committee of sergeants. "A total dissolution of the Pennsylvania Line—or an order to disband the whole—is more advisable than to admit the unreasonable claims of these mutineers," he declared.

By January 12, Wayne was in Trenton, New Jersey, reporting that the soldiers had ended the mutiny. To demonstrate that they were dissatisfied, but not disloyal, the mutineers had arrested Clinton's agents and turned them over to Wayne, who promptly had them tried for espionage.

"The two spies were executed yesterday," Wayne told Washington.

By May, the soldiers of the Pennsylvania Line were encamped at York, Pennsylvania, preparing for what became an overland march of two hundred and seventy miles to Yorktown, Virginia. The events of January had all but become ancient history. Many veterans, their three-year enlistments up, had been discharged. Early in the war, there had been fifteen Pennsylvania regiments and ten battalions. These numbers had fluctuated somewhat as the Revolution progressed, but after the mutiny, the line had been consolidated, and its officers had dispersed throughout the state to recruit fresh troops.

In spring came orders for the Pennsylvanians to join other Continental forces in the south. "All the recruits fit for service, from the different stations, were brought to York, formed into two regiments of eight companies each, destined for the State of Virginia," said Lieutenant Ebenezer Denny, a soldier from Carlisle.

But then, suddenly, in late May, as they prepared for the long march to Virginia, the soldiers in the newly reorganized regiments at York mutinied over money. Inflation had nearly wrecked the currency in which Pennsylvania paid its soldiers. Conflict set in when auditors charged with paying the troops distributed money that "was not equal to one-seventh part of its nominal value," General Wayne said later. "This was an alarming circumstance."

When the soldiers attempted to use the money to purchase goods from York merchants, the merchants declined to sell, "saying it was not worth accepting," the general said. The townspeople made matters worse when they told the soldiers "that they ought not to march until justice was done them."

Presently, "a few leading mutineers on the right of each regiment called out to pay them in real and not ideal money: they were no longer to be trifled with," Wayne said.

The officers ordered their men to their tents, but the men refused to go. When this happened, "the principals were immediately either knocked down or confined by the officers, who were previously prepared for this event," the general said.

Wayne immediately convened a court-martial. In a May 20 letter, Wayne said: "The determined countenances of the officers produced a conviction to the soldiery that the sentence of the court-martial would be carried into execution at every risk and consequence."

As Lieutenant Denny, who served in the 4th Pennsylvania, wrote in his journal: "Twenty-odd prisoners (were) brought before them; seven were sentenced to die."

"Earlier than usual," the regiments formed for the evening parade, Denny said. "Orders passed to the officers along the line to put to death instantly any man who stirred from his rank. In front of the parade, the ground rose and descended again, and at the distance of about three hundred yards over this rising ground, the prisoners were escorted by a captain's guard."

Standing at the parade ground, the rank-and-file soldiers "heard the fire of one platoon and immediately a smaller one." Within minutes, "the regiments wheeled by companies and marched round by the place of execution. This was an awful exhibition. The seven objects were seen by the troops just as they had sunk or fell under the fire."

As General Wayne remarked in the letter, "Whether by design or accident, the particular friends and messmates of the culprits were their executioners, and while the tears rolled down their cheeks in showers, they silently and faithfully obeyed their orders without a moment's hesitation."

He added, "Thus was this hideous monster crushed in its birth, however, to myself and officers a most painful scene."

On May 26, the troops marched south. "This day, we left York at 9 o'clock in the morning with about eight hundred effective men under the command of General Wayne and encamped eleven miles on the road to Frederick Town," wrote Lieutenant William McDowell of the 1st

Pennsylvania Regiment. The Pennsylvania regiments belonged to the overall command of the Marquis de Lafayette.

Wayne had orders to join Lafayette, who had taken his army to eastern Virginia, where a dangerous situation had developed. In late May, Lafayette reported to Washington that Cornwallis had brought an English army into southern Virginia from North Carolina. At Petersburg, nearly twenty-five miles south of Richmond, Cornwallis had linked up with a British army led by General Benedict Arnold, who had marched west from the Chesapeake Bay.

Washington wanted Lafayette to watch the British closely, but in a June 4 letter from New Windsor, New York, instructed the Frenchman: "not to hazard before nor after your junction with General Wayne a general action unless you have very sure grounds to do it on."

As Thomas Jefferson, then in his final days as governor of Virginia, reported to Washington, according to "the best intelligence I have been able to get," the British had seven thousand troops—infantry and cavalry—in Virginia. The figure included "a reinforcement of two thousand men just arrived from New York." These soldiers had crossed the James River, and by May 26, had begun moving towards Richmond. In contrast, the marquis waited for the British at Richmond with a mere three thousand men, "regulars and militia," Jefferson said.

The two Pennsylvania regiments knew little of this as they headed south of the Mason-Dixon Line on a route that took them through Taneytown, Monocacy, Frederick Town, and Leesburg.

After a day's march on May 29, the 1st Pennsylvania camped on the north side of the Monocacy River, a tributary of the Potomac, and spent the next day in camp. "The soldiers washed themselves and scoured up their arms and accouterments," Lieutenant McDowell wrote. "At 7 o'clock, they were reviewed by General Wayne."

On May 31st, the troops "took up the line of march at sunrise (and) passed through Frederick, Maryland, where there were a number of British officers, prisoners of war, who took a view of us as we passed through the town," McDowell said. "We made a very respectable appearance."

The Pennsylvanians made eighteen miles that day and crossed the Potomac at a place McDowell called Noland's Ferry: "We . . . were obliged to cross in bad boats. One unfortunately sunk . . . and . . . one sergeant and three men of our regiment were drowned."

When it sunk, the ferry was "loaded with artillery, quartermaster stores, and men," according to Captain John Davis of the 1st Pennsylvania.

The accident may have slowed but didn't stop the crossing. The men camped on the Potomac's south side. "A number of us dined at the tavern, or ordinary, as the Virginians call it," McDowell said. "The night proved bad, and we could not pitch our tents."

The weather of early June became "very wet and disagreeable," McDowell said. On June 4, for example, the men "marched through a low country, roads being very bad in consequence of the rains we had a few days before."

On June 8, the soldiers waded across the North Branch of Rappahannock. On the 9th, they crossed the Rappahannock's South Branch.

As Wayne hurriedly marched his troops a hundred and fifty miles nearly due south, Lafayette found himself confronting Cornwallis in southern Virginia.

"General Washington wrote to Lafayette that he could send him no other reinforcement than eight hundred of the mutinous Pennsylvanians," Lafayette said in his memoirs, published posthumously in 1837. In contrast, "The active corps of Cornwallis was composed of more than four thousand men, of which eight hundred were supplied with horses."

At one point, the Frenchman came into possession of an intercepted letter that Cornwallis had written, in which he boasted, "The boy cannot escape me."

As it turned out, Cornwallis caught neither the boy nor his army, which Lafayette, writing in the third person, described as his "little corps, who, including recruits and the militia, did not exceed two thousand five hundred men. The richest young men of Virginia and Maryland had come to join him as volunteer dragoons, and from their intelligence, as well as from the superiority of their horses, they had been of essential service to him."

Meanwhile, Lafayette said, "Wayne was advancing with the reinforcement of Pennsylvanians. Lafayette made all his calculations so as to be able to effect a junction with that corps, without being prevented from covering the military magazines of the southern states, which were at the foot of the mountains on the height of Fluvanna (west of Richmond in the Virginia piedmont). But the Pennsylvanians had delayed their movements." Although the delay complicated Lafayette's situation, the two forces eventually joined up.

The June 10 march of the Pennsylvanians began at 5 a.m.. During "a very severe march of twenty-three miles," McDowell reported, the 1st Pennsylvania "joined the Marquis's troops this day and passed a body of militia of Virginia about eighteen hundred men."

On June 12, the soldiers "marched through a thicket of pine woods, nothing but a footpath through which we got with great difficulty, especially our artillery," McDowell said. "At last, we arrived at the main road leading to Fredericksburg, which I long looked for, and encamped five miles from where we entered the road."

June 14 saw the 1st Pennsylvania marching "through poor country, the water being very scarce," McDowell said. Along the way, they saw "a number of Negroes, the greatest part of them being naked."

The 15th was remarkably dry. "A great scarcity of water this day and a very fatiguing march," McDowell said. "Refreshed ourselves in an orchard . . . Colonel Robinson, the Marquis, and General Wayne took a bite with us."

The 4th Pennsylvania caught up with Lafayette a few days later. Lieutenant Denny reported in his journal entry for June 18 that the regiment "joined the troops under command of Lafayette. The marquis had marched two or three days to meet us. His men look as if they were fit for business. They are chiefly all light infantry, dressed in frocks and overalls of linen."

June 18 treated the soldiers to "a sweet morning," but it also provided tension because "this day the enemy advanced on us," Captain Davis said. "Our camp struck at sunset. All the Continental troops marched in order to surprise a party of horse. We continued till day, but on our arrival where they were, they had gone some hours."

McDowell discovered that Virginia women were curious about the northern soldiers. "They sometimes come to the roadside in order to take a view of us as we pass the road," he wrote as the regiment approached Richmond on June 22. "A person can scarcely discern any part of their face, but their nose and eyes, as they have themselves muffled with linen in order to prevent the sun from burning their fair faces."

McDowell noted a contradiction: "At the same time, they will have a number of blacks all naked around them, nothing to cover their nakedness."

The Pennsylvanians encountered reports of enemy activity as they approached Richmond, "where Lord Cornwallis with the British army lay," Lieutenant Denny wrote. "Heard that his lordship was employed burning and destroying warehouses of tobacco."

Lieutenant McDowell's June 22 journal entry noted, "We passed through Richmond twenty-four hours after the enemy evacuated it, a number of horses being destroyed by them. They also destroyed a quantity of tobacco, which they threw into the street and set on fire. The town is built close on James River under a bank."

On June 22, the 1st Pennsylvania camped two miles south of Richmond. It broke camp and at 2 a.m. on June 23, set out on a night march. The regiment halted for refreshment at 8 o'clock, McDowell said. Suddenly, "our light horse brought intelligence, the enemy was within one mile of us. The army immediately formed for action. A universal joy prevailed . . . we lay on our arms ten hours, hourly waiting for action . . . , but to our mortification, (it) turned out a false alarm," he said.

On June 24, a soldier belonging to the 4th Pennsylvania was caught attempting to desert to the British. McDowell reported, "At 3 o'clock, p.m., he was tried and sentenced to be shot, which punishment was inflicted on him at retreat beat" as the camp closed up for the night.

On June 26, the Continentals discovered British cavalry a short distance in front of them. "General Wayne . . . ordered the front platoons of each battalion to turn out immediately," McDowell said. ". . . We pursued them for five or six miles in full speed. At last, we came within a short distance of them."

New Jersey dragoons and Pennsylvania infantrymen "soon overtook them," McDowell said afterward. "We had a skirmish with their horse and infantry in which we took a number of their horse and cattle and killed forty of their infantry. Our loss was very inconsiderable. Major McPherson's horse threw him in the field of action, but fortunately made his escape."

The Continentals reached the York River on July 1, and time was allotted "for the troops to wash and refresh themselves," McDowell said.

The Pennsylvanians entered the forty-mile-long peninsula situated between the James and York rivers. They soon learned they were behind a British force that was moving down the peninsula, with a rear guard of horse soldiers herding "a great number of cattle." They were led by a colonel, "plundering as he was making his way to Jamestown," McDowell said.

The Americans came upon "one Negro man with the small pox laying on the roadside." The lieutenant speculated that the British had deliberately left him there "in order to prevent the Virginia Militia from pursuing them."

By nightfall of July 5, the soldiers had reached a place called Chickahominy Church, "where we lay on our arms till sunrise," McDowell said.

At sunup on the 6th, "we took up the line of march for Jamestown, at which place the enemy lay encamped. The first battalion of our line were detached with a small party of riflemen, which brought on a scattering fire in front, and on the flank of our battalion that continued for two or three hours with the Yagers.

"Our battalion was then ordered to form column and advance," McDowell said.

British troops came in view as the Pennsylvanians moved forward. "Our advance was regular, and at a charge, till we came within eighty yards of the whole army, they being regularly formed standing at one yard's distance from each other, their light infantry being in front of our battalion," McDowell said. "We advanced under a very heavy fire of grape shot at which distance we opened our musketry, but being overpowered, were obliged to retreat with precipitation, and in bad order for at least one mile, where we formed and retired in good order."

The British didn't pursue as the Americans withdrew. "Happy for us," McDowell said, "the enemy did not press us at this critical moment, or our troops would have inevitably been cut off. We retired to Chickahominy Church about eight miles where a number of the officers' wounds were dressed, and all the privates who were wounded, it being at this time about 10 o'clock at night."

Events taking place around this time along the Hudson River in New York had a significant impact on the Pennsylvanians over the next several months. Washington had learned that a French fleet had reached North America, and he needed to inform Lafayette as rapidly as possible.

Writing to General Samuel Miles, a Pennsylvanian who was deputy quartermaster general, on August 15, Washington said, "The enclosed dispatches for the Marquis De La Fayette are of the greatest importance . . . I must request you will forward the letter immediately by a trusty, active express, with orders to ride night and day, and to call on the magistrates or military officers for horses and assistance; and to deliver the letter to the Marquis at the earliest possible period."

Writing from Chatham, New Jersey, on August 27, Washington advised the president of Congress, a Pennsylvanian named Thomas McKean, "I am now on my march

The York River beach at Yorktown. The bridge at far left leads to Gloucester.

with a very considerable detachment of the American army and the whole of the French troops for Virginia."

As August ended, the Hessians and British with Lord Cornwallis had settled in at Yorktown, a village on a hillside that overlooked the mouth of the York River, beyond which lay the Chesapeake Bay and, beyond that, the Atlantic.

At sunrise on September 1, an express rider raced past the Pennsylvania troops as he headed for Lafayette, who was camped along the Pamunkey River, a tributary of the York. The rider had come from the lower Chesapeake Bay with news that Count de Grasse, the French admiral, had arrived off Hampton Roads the day before. His fleet of thirty-two ships had come from the Caribbean. It included twenty-eight ships of the line and four frigates. Lieutenant Colonel Richard Butler, who commanded a battalion of Pennsylvanians, noted in his journal that the ships had already reached "the bay of Chesapeake, with seven thousand troops, ready to act in conjunction with the American army."

Lafayette relayed this news to Washington the same day. He added that "Lord Cornwallis is still on York River and is fortifying himself in a strong position." Even so, Lafayette's forces had taken such positions "as to prevent the enemy's retreating towards Carolina."

In his memoirs, Lafayette said that his "principal object had been to force Lord Cornwallis to withdraw towards the seashore, and then entangle him in such a manner in the rivers that there should remain no possibility of a retreat. The English, on the contrary, fancied themselves in a very good position, as they were possessors of a seaport."

Cornwallis simply had to wait for the British fleet to sail in from the Atlantic Ocean and then transport his army to New York or some other British-held port.

By late afternoon of the 1st, Butler's column had reached Surry, Virginia, on the south side of the James River. As the crow flies, Surry was about twenty miles southwest of Yorktown. He went down to the river "to see if any of the French ships had got up." He soon found himself "directly opposite to Jamestown and island, the river a league (about three miles) wide . . . a very good prospect up and down the river."

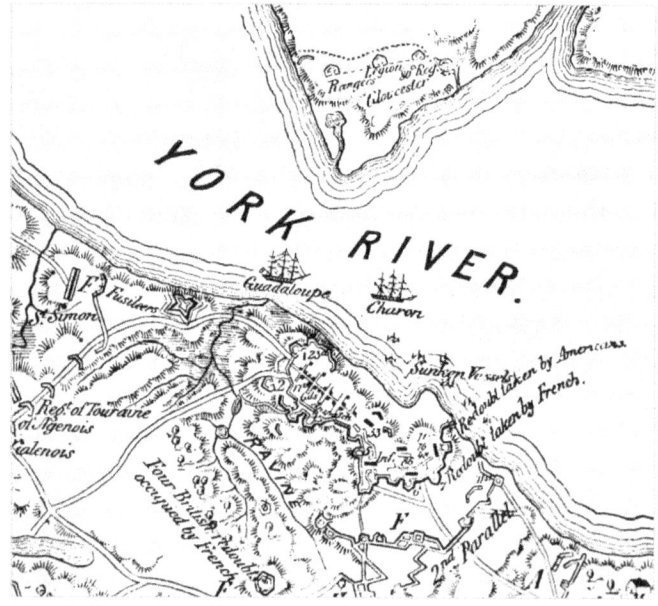

Detail of map shows Yorktown in the center, just below the York River. American and French forces occupied the areas on the left and in the foreground. British-held Gloucester was on a point of land across the river.

A little later, Butler and another senior officer, Colonel Walter Stewart, went several miles farther east—well beyond a point that had obstructed their view. "We were overjoyed to see the Experiment, a French forty-gun ship, and four frigates at anchor," Butler said. There were also "three prize vessels, taken on their way to this coast." Butler counted an additional "forty large boats, with near four thousand troops, coming up the bay." The soldiers had come to Virginia aboard the French fleet, which lay at anchor in Hampton Roads.

It was midnight by the time Butler and Stewart returned to General Wayne's quarters "with these pleasing accounts, all of which was immediately communicated to the officers, whose joy was great and their happiness expressed by every mark of joy and pleasure."

A German soldier from Bavaria, Corporal Stephan Popp, was twenty-two when his regiment sailed to North America in March 1777 to assist the British in putting down the American rebellion. As he traveled, Popp kept a journal of his experiences. On April 7, for instance, his regiment departed Portsmouth, England, bound for New York in a fleet of sixteen ships escorted by a British warship with seventy-four guns.

"We reached the harbor of New York, after much stormy weather on the voyage," on June 3, Popp wrote. The next day, "the birthday of King George the III was celebrated by guns fired on all the men-of-war and ships in the harbor, over three hundred in all," Popp wrote.

Four years later, Popp's regiment remained in North America. As the war shifted to Virginia in 1781, Popp and his comrades were sent there from New York. "Landed at

Norfolk and pitched our camp at Portsmouth," he wrote on May 27. "Plenty of fish and oysters, and caught crabs . . . Norfolk was a pretty town, but it was burned down by the rebels."

On June 11, he reported, "A Negro was arrested for poisoning our wells, by his master's order, who escaped. Many of the English soldiers died. In Portsmouth, Lord Cornwallis had over a thousand Negroes, employed to cut wood, work on the trenches, etc."

In late July, Popp and his comrades were sent to the lower York River, where their ship anchored off Yorktown, which he called "a little village." He noted that "most of the owners of the houses had left them."

The Germans landed and went into camp on August 1. "Lord Cornwallis was already here with most of his army, only a small force left in Portsmouth," Popp said.

The British and the Germans devoted much of August to digging trenches and throwing up defensive lines at both Yorktown and Gloucester, opposite Yorktown, on the point of land on the York River's eastern shore. As Popp noted ominously on August 24, "there are reports that we are in a very bad situation."

Two days later, "a French fleet has arrived from the West Indies, men-of-war and transports with troops," the corporal noted. "Day and night, we are at work strengthening our lines, have hardly time to eat, and little food, but we are getting ready to make a stout defense."

As August ended, the French ships had placed themselves "in full view" of Cornwallis' army as they "landed many troops from Rhode Island." There was another significant development: "French soldiers and rebels are

From York to Yorktown 63

French ships blocked the Chesapeake Bay and prevented the British navy from rescuing General Cornwallis and his army.

marching from the James River and Williamsburg," Popp wrote. "We are in daily expectation of an attack by land and by water. Our ships landed all their stores, their guns put on our lines, fire ships got ready, every preparation made as rapidly as possible."

On September 2, the Pennsylvanians marched about six miles to Cobham Point, on the south side of the James River, "where we encamped, and about 1 o'clock saw, with pleasure, the (French) boats come up and land on James Island, covered by the three prize vessels," Butler said.

General Wayne took Butler, Stewart, and several other officers across the James to the French camp near Jamestown, not quite twenty miles west of Yorktown. "We requested boats for the crossing of our troops, which were given with the greatest cheerfulness, and after mutual compliments passed, we re-crossed," Butler said.

Wayne remained on the north shore. He had had an appointment to meet with Lafayette, and a sentry had accidentally shot him in the thigh. "The wound is not dangerous," Butler reported. Nonetheless, Wayne remained in the French camp to convalesce.

The French admiral, the Count de Grasse, soon sailed up the York River and blockaded Yorktown. As Lafayette reported, when an English fleet commanded by Admiral Thomas Graves appeared off the Chesapeake in early September, the count left several ships necessary for maintaining the blockade, "and, having gone out of the harbor to attack Admiral Graves, forced the English to retire, and returned to his former station in the bay."

By mid-September, excitement grew throughout the American camp at Williamsburg in the expectation that the commander-in-chief would soon appear. Finally, on the 14th, a "twenty-one gun firing announced the arrival of General Washington in camp," wrote Captain Davis of the 1st Pennsylvania. "The army paraded and was reviewed before he lighted from his horse."

Finding Cornwallis well entrenched on the high ground above Yorktown, the Americans prepared to besiege the town. They began by digging trenches that ran parallel to—but outside of—the British defenses. Although they worked during the day, they also worked at night when darkness reduced their vulnerability to enemy guns.

Captain Davis detailed how the British and Hessians withdrew to inside their defenses and relied on their artillery to harass their besiegers. On October 1, "a warm fire continued all day, about forty guns to the hour on an average, and ten by night to the hour," Davis said. "Two men only killed, one of them in the works."

On the 2nd, the captain reported "a continual firing from the enemy's batteries all this day." Even so, the firing didn't stop the French and Americans from constructing the earthworks they needed to carry out the siege. "Our works goes on rapidly," Davis said.

On the 3rd, the British artillerymen gained a temporary advantage. "A deserter went in who informed them where our covering parties lay," Davis said. "They directed their shot for them. The first killed three men and mortally wounded a fourth." Nonetheless, "our works go on rapidly."

Not every American soldier respected the abilities of the British artillerymen. "A militiaman this day," wrote Captain James Duncan, ". . . constantly stood on the parapet and d—d his soul if he would dodge for the buggers. He had escaped longer than could have been expected, and, growing fool-hardy, brandished his spade at every ball that was fired, till, unfortunately, a ball came and put an end to his capers."

French and American regiments devoted the night of October 6 to digging a trench along a "line (that) extends itself to the river on each side the town, and at all places nearly equally distant and better than two hundred yards in front of the former works," reported Duncan, who served in Colonel Moses Hazen's Regiment. "The enemy discovered us although the night was pretty favorable, but the chief of their fire was directed against the French."

By daybreak on October 7, the Americans had dug "trenches so deep that we could sustain little or no harm from their fire," Duncan said. He speculated that the British "were, no doubt, much astonished in the morning to find themselves so completely hemmed in on all sides."

By October 10, the allies had their guns in position. "Last night commenced a very heavy cannonade, and the enemy returned the fire with no less spirit," the captain wrote on October 11. ". . . The whole night was nothing but one continual roar of cannon, mixed with the bursting of shells and rumbling of houses torn to pieces."

Duncan reported that the largest British ship in the harbor "was set on fire by the bursting of a shell or red-hot ball from some of our batteries." The blaze spread to a nearby ship, and "both . . . were burnt down. They must have lost a considerable amount of powder . . . as there was an explosion which made a heavy report."

The October 12 diary entry of Lieutenant William Feltman of the 1st Pennsylvania Regiment explains how the soldiers dug the trenches:

"Last evening at 5 a detachment from our division was ordered on fatigue in order to run the second parallel . . . I had the honor to be one of the number and had a command of eighty-two men and another officer with me. Every second man of the whole detachment carried a fascine and shovel or a spade, and every man a shovel, a spade, or grubbing hoe."

American and French artillery along this line bombarded British positions in Yorktown.

Fascines were a type of prefabricated building material. They consisted of long sticks bundled together and tied with twine or rope. In constructing the Yorktown earthworks, Continental soldiers placed them on the British side of the new trenches, then covered them with dirt to help in stopping the incoming enemy fire.

"Just at dusk, we advanced within gunshot of the enemy, then began our work," Feltman said. "In one hour's time, we had ourselves completely covered, so we disregarded their cannonading. They discharged a number of pieces at our party, but they had little effect. They only wounded one of our men. We were in the center of two fires, from the enemy and our own. But the latter was very dangerous. We had two men killed and one badly wounded from the French batteries. Also, a number of shells burst in the air above our heads, which was very dangerous to us. We dug the ditch three and a half feet deep and seven feet in width. In the morning before daylight, we were relieved by the militia."

The British had constructed two redoubts on the far left of their defensive line. By mid-October, the allies decided the time had come to silence the British guns positioned in these posts. "Last evening just at dark," Lieutenant Feltman wrote on October 15, "two of our regiments of light Infantry under the command of the Marquis de Lafayette came to the trenches. Immediately after, they advanced toward the enemy's out-works, which they stormed and carried with success with the loss of a few killed and wounded. . . . The French carried one work and our infantry another."

Captain Duncan added additional details: "A little before dark . . . every man was ordered to disencumber himself of his pack. The evening was pretty dark and favored the attack. The column advanced, Colonel Guinot's regiment in front and ours in the rear. We had not got far before we were discovered, and now the enemy opened a fire of cannon, grapeshot, shell, and musketry upon us, but all to no effect. The column moved on undisturbed and took the redoubt by the bayonet without firing a single gun."

Later in the day, "we completed our second parallel line. . . . Our second parallel line is now within two hundred and fifty yards of the enemy's main works, which is Yorktown," Feltman said. ". . . We have a fine prospect of the town, river, and the enemy's shipping . . . Upon the right of our line, we are erecting a twelve-gun battery."

The end of the siege was approaching. The Americans had no way of knowing it, but Cornwallis had managed to maintain communications with Sir Henry Clinton in New York throughout September and into October. Their

Americans cannonade British positions at Yorktown.

letters reveal that as early as September 16, Cornwallis was worried. "The enemy's fleet has returned," His Lordship advised Sir Henry. "Two line of battle ships and one frigate lie at the mouth of this river; and three or four line of battle ships, several frigates, and transports went up the (Chesapeake) bay on 12th and 14th."

Cornwallis said, "This place is in no state of defense. If you can not relieve me very soon, you must be prepared to hear the worst." He noted that food supplies were beginning to run low and that he was considering the possibility of expelling all non-combatants. "By . . . turning out useless mouths, my provisions will last six weeks from this day, if we can preserve them from accidents."

The general added, "I hear Washington arrived at Williamsburg on the 14th."

Although the distance between Yorktown and Manhattan was less than four hundred miles, it took more than a week for Cornwallis' letter to reach Clinton, who replied on September 24. Clinton said he would send a fleet of twenty-three "sail of the line, three of which are three-deckers," to relieve Yorktown.

"There is every reason to hope we start from hence the 5th of October," Clinton said.

Clinton's letter reached Cornwallis five days later, and Cornwallis dashed off a brief reply. "I . . . have no doubt if relief arrives in any reasonable time, York(town) and Gloucester will be both in possession of His Majesty's troops." He added, "medicines are wanted."

The British had a garrison at Gloucester Point, directly across the York from Yorktown.

Cornwallis's October 3 letter informed his commander that due to "the uncommon exertions of the troops, our works are in a better state of defense than we had reason to hope." He also reported, "the enemy are encamped about two miles from us. On the night of the 30th of September, they broke ground and made two redoubts about eleven hundred yards from our works. . . . They have finished these redoubts, and I expect they will go on with their works this night."

On October 10, Cornwallis received Clinton's September 30th letter: "I am doing everything in my power to relieve you."

On October 11, Cornwallis reported that American and French artillery had begun bombarding British positions "and have since continued firing without intermission, with about forty cannon, mostly heavy, and sixteen mortars, from eight to sixteen inches." Casualties were mounting. "We have lost about seventy men, and many of our works are considerably damaged . . . one cannot hope to make a very long resistance." The allies were firing from an offensive line that ran parallel to the British defensive line "at the distance of six hundred yards," he said. But this changed dramatically. "Last night," Cornwallis said on October 12, "the enemy made their second parallel at the distance of three hundred yards. We continue to lose men very fast."

The British managed to hold out for another five days. Then, on October 17, "at 10 o'clock, a.m., Lord Cornwallis sent out a flag, requesting a suspension of hostilities for twenty-four hours," Colonel Butler reported.

Lieutenant Denny of the 4th Pennsylvania described the scene as the fighting suddenly ended. "In the morning," he had "had the pleasure of seeing a drummer mount the enemy's parapet, and beat a parley, and immediately an officer, holding up a white handkerchief, made his appearance outside their works. The drummer accompanied him, beating.

"Our batteries ceased. An officer from our lines ran and met the other, and tied the handkerchief over his eyes. The drummer sent back, and the British officer (was) conducted to a house in rear of our lines. Firing ceased totally."

Denny continued: "Had we not seen the drummer in his red coat when he first mounted, he might have beat away till doomsday. The constant firing was too much for the sound of a single drum, but when the firing ceased, I thought I never heard a drum equal to it—the most delightful music to us all."

Washington didn't reply to Cornwallis' request for a twenty-four-hour ceasefire. "About 4 o'clock, p.m., another flag (appeared), requesting a cessation for four hours,"

The Moore House, Yorktown, where surrender terms were negotiated in October 1781.

Colonel Butler reported. This time "the general agreed that a cessation should take place for two hours."

On October 18, American and British officers negotiated the surrender. "The troops in the trenches being entitled to the honor of closing the siege, we, therefore, remained unrelieved in the trenches," Butler reported. "This day, the whole army were ordered to hold themselves in readiness for any service requisite." That way, if the talks broke down, the Americans could resume fighting immediately.

On October 19, Butler wrote, "About 11 o'clock, a.m., all settled, the capitulation was signed . . . then the two armies were drawn up opposite to each other, on the road leading from York to the country, and at 2 p.m., the British army marched out, to the great satisfaction of the whole American army and all spectators."

On the 19th, "All is quiet," reported Lieutenant Denny.

With the articles of capitulation signed, detachments of French and Americans took possession of British defenses. Denny described the day's events:

"I carried the standard of our regiment on this occasion. On entering the fort, Baron Steuben, who accompanied us, took the standard from me and planted it himself.

"The British army parade and march out with their colors furled. Drums beat as if they did not care how. Grounded their arms and returned to town.

"Much confusion and riot among the British through the day. Many of the soldiers were intoxicated. Several attempts in course of the night to break open stores. An American sentinel killed by a British soldier with a bayonet. Our patrols kept busy.

"Glad to be relieved from this disagreeable station. Negroes lie about, sick and dying, in every stage of the small pox.

"Never was in so filthy a place—some handsome houses, but prodigiously shattered. Vast heaps of shot and shells lying about in every quarter, which came from our works. The shells did not burst, as was expected."

The Americans found that the British had a "fine supply of stores and merchandise," Denny said. ". . . Articles suitable for clothing were taken for the use of the army."

Summer 1776

Prisoners of war

The Americans captured Johannes Schwalm, a Hessian infantryman, twice.

Born in May 1749 in Germany's Schwalm River Valley in the state of Hesse-Kassel, Schwalm was twenty-seven years old and a private in the Regiment von Knyphausen when he and thousands of other German soldiers arrived in North America—more specifically, Staten Island in New York Harbor—in August 1776.

Although Americans tended to refer to all German troops as Hessians, they included soldiers from such other German principalities as Waldeck and Brunswick. They came as auxiliaries, not mercenaries.

Within months, Schwalm found himself among the nine hundred Hessians captured by General George Washington's Continental Army at Trenton, New Jersey, on the day after Christmas 1776.

Schwalm and his fellow prisoners were soon taken across the icy Delaware River to Pennsylvania, detained briefly at the village church in Newtown, escorted to Philadelphia where they were paraded through the streets, and then marched off to a prison camp at Lancaster some seventy miles to the west.

The illustration depicts Johannes Schwalm, a Hessian soldier captured at Trenton in 1776.

In late summer of 1777, when it seemed certain that a British fleet had sailed into the upper Chesapeake Bay and would likely invade southeastern Pennsylvania, hundreds of Hessian POWs were moved thirty miles north to Lebanon. They were returned when the British occupied Philadelphia, about seventy miles to the east.

German prisoners were also kept at Reading, some thirty miles northeast of Lancaster. Following the Battle of Trenton, some Hessians were also sent to Reading, about sixty-five miles northwest of Philadelphia. As 19th-century historian I.D. Rupp reported in his 1844 *History of the Counties of Berks and Lebanon*, the prisoners "built themselves huts in regular camp order." Located on a hill east of Reading, the settlement became known locally as "the Hessian Camp."

The life of German prisoners in the Pennsylvania countryside wasn't necessarily harsh. Many Germans had settled in Lancaster County before the Revolution, and many prisoners managed to obtain jobs on farms owned by Germans. Surviving documentation suggests that Johannes Schwalm may have found work for a German who operated both a distillery and a tavern.

A Hessian soldier

Some German POWs also found more specialized types of work. In March 1778, for instance, word spread through Lancaster that prisoners belonging to "a Hessian band" were being paid—"fifteen pounds for each night's attendance"—to perform at community dances, or so retired druggist Christopher Marshall noted in his journal.

Hundreds of German prisoners were exchanged during 1778. Schwalm was released in June and sent to New York, where he rejoined his regiment near Harlem on Manhattan, which had been under British control since September 1776.

Schwalm's second capture occurred in September 1779. One of a hundred and sixty soldiers bound for Canada, he was aboard a small ship, *The Molly*, which had sailed from New York. It belonged to a convoy of twenty-two troop ships transporting Hessian and British soldiers to Quebec. The fleet assembled in Lower New York Bay and, with an escort of British warships, sailed into the Atlantic on September 11.

On the 15th, a hurricane scattered the fleet and blew the ships far off course. Two transports were lost in the storm. Days later, American privateers captured *The Molly* off the coast of New Jersey and took her up the Delaware River to Philadelphia, where she arrived on September 28. Her contents were sold at auction, and Schwalm and his comrades were confined in the city's new jail.

They were among the thousands of German soldiers—some accompanied by wives and children—who lived in American jails and prison camps during the war.

October 1777: Capturing the Convention Army

German soldiers represented a significant element in the British army that left Quebec in 1777 and marched more than three hundred miles south to the Hudson River Valley in New York State. General John Burgoyne, its commander, intended to conquer the Hudson Valley in a move that would sever New England from the rebellious country's Mid-Atlantic and Southern regions.

As recounted in the 1957 classic, *Rebels & Redcoats*, Burgoyne's force consisted of more than eight thousand three hundred soldiers "including six hundred artillerymen for a train of one hundred thirty-eight guns, six hundred fifty Canadian and Tory auxiliaries, four hundred Indians of the Six Nations, and a main force of three thousand seven hundred smartly-trained (British) regulars and three thousand Germans, almost all of the latter Brunswickers."

Supplementing Burgoyne's army were four hundred British, Germans, and Tories that Lieutenant Colonel Barry St. Leger brought down New York's Mohawk River from Montreal. Many Iroquois warriors joined them so that St. Leger's command exceeded a thousand men.

Burgoyne's expedition failed spectacularly. St. Leger's early August siege of Fort Schuyler along the Mohawk River at present-day Rome, New York, resulted in an American victory when the British abandoned the siege and fled. In mid-August, American militia troops defeated seven hundred troops that Burgoyne had sent to raid Bennington, Vermont.

Although Burgoyne in mid-September defeated the Americans at Freeman's Farm near Saratoga, in early October, he was defeated in a second battle, this one on Bemis Heights along the Hudson River. Unable to retreat, the general surrendered his entire army. The terms of the surrender were called a convention, and Burgoyne's army became known as the Convention Army. The agreement called for the defeated soldiers to march to Boston, where British ships would take them back to Europe.

The Convention Army made the two hundred-mile march to Cambridge, Massachusetts, by early November, but the prisoners never sailed for Europe. Instead, the U.S. Congress revoked the agreement in January 1778 and kept the prisoners in Cambridge for most of the year. That November, the POWs were marched to Charlottesville,

Virginia, more than five hundred miles to the south. The trek took two months.

June 1779: French woman travels on the sly

During the war, travelers leaving Philadelphia for New York often took a combination of boats, carriages, and stagecoaches that took them on a thirty-mile boat trip up the Delaware River to Bordentown, New Jersey; then across a forty-mile stretch of central New Jersey by stagecoach to Perth Amboy on Raritan Bay; and finally for a second boat ride, this one across the Hudson River to Manhattan, a distance of about thirty miles.

Most interstate travelers were required to obtain passes that allowed them to cross state borders, but a Canadian woman, Charlotte Latima, in a chance meeting with William Livingston, the governor of New Jersey, boasted that she had skipped that step.

"I met accidentally with a lady last evening, that, among a multitude of other passengers, had just landed here out of the stage boat from Philadelphia," Livingston said in a letter written at Bordentown on June 7, 1779.

Latima told Livingston that she managed to travel "without a pass from any state." The governor added, "She acknowledges herself bound for New York after she shall have stayed at Amboy as long she thinks proper."

Livingston addressed his letter to Joseph Reed, president of the Pennsylvania Supreme Executive Council, in Philadelphia. He explained that he was sending Mrs. Latima back to Pennsylvania. "Your Excellency, upon her further examination, may either think proper to send her along further southward or, in case she may only be permitted to

Wives and children often accompanied Hessian soldiers during the Revolution.

go to New York, to grant her your pass, according to the resolve of Congress."

The woman had told Livingston that she had been on the move ever since October 1777, when the Continental Army defeated General John Burgoyne at Saratoga, New York. Becoming known as the Convention Army, these prisoners were first marched from Saratoga to Massachusetts and later to Virginia.

"She pretends to have been taken with Burgoyne's army, in which she says that her husband, a Canadian, fell; and that she has a brother in the British service in New York with the Convention Prisoners," Livingston wrote. "She says she marched to Virginia, and has travelled thence to this place without a pass from any state."

He added, "I take her to be one of their female news carriers, and have sent her back to the last state she came from. She confessed to the passengers in the boat that she had been both at Quebec and New York since the surrender of Burgoyne."

Five days later, Livingston again wrote to Reed, this time from Trenton, regarding Mrs. Latima, whom he described as "the prisoner herewith sent (to) you."

The governor explained that she had arrived in Bordentown on June 6. "As soon as she landed, she deposited her trunks with one Watson, a notorious Tory, and then came to the tavern where I ordered her to be kept till she would be sent back to Philadelphia."

But Mrs. Latima had other plans. "She escaped from thence and was apprehended on her way to New York and brought to this place. From hence she again made her escape and was again apprehended," Livingston said.

The governor described Mrs. Latima as a spirited woman. "She protests she will go to New York in defiance of all men, and appears to me extremely well calculated for, and is doubtless employed in, carrying dispatches for the enemy," he said.

"The papers found upon her, I enclose, which seem of no good consequence. Probably Your Excellency will think proper to send her along to Virginia where she left the Convention Troops, or confine her in Philadelphia till she is better known."

A search of her baggage and handbag had turned up some interesting material. "She appears by some memoranda in her pocketbook to be a very great traveler, and, by one of the letters, to have lodged some time with Mr.

Dayman in Philadelphia, who will doubtless be able to give some account of her."

By mid-June, Mrs. Latima was incarcerated in Philadelphia. As Reed reported to Livingston on June 17, "The French woman was brought before me, and after making inquiry of persons in this city respecting her, the result was so unfavorable that I sent her to the state prison . . ."

Pennsylvania authorities issued passes sparingly. "We give but few papers and to none but those who give security not to return to this state without leave first obtained for that purpose," Reed said. He added that people occasionally managed to leave Pennsylvania and travel to New York surreptitiously. "They go from this (state) under pretense of going to New Jersey and there proceed by the stages," he said.

Charlotte Latima would remain in prison "till the next exchange of prisoners by which time any Intelligence she can carry must be stale and of little value," Reed said.

After this mention, she disappears from the record.

March 1781: POWs moved to Pennsylvania

When British armies invaded eastern Virginia in 1781, the prisoners were moved again.

In March 1781, the U.S. Board of War ordered that all British and Hessians being held in Virginia and Maryland be transferred north: "the British to Yorktown (modern-day York) and the Germans to Lancaster town in . . . Pennsylvania, or such other place or places within the said state."

For the Hessians held at Charlottesville, this meant another march of more than two hundred miles, this time to Lancaster.

In late December 1776, Hessian officers taken prisoner at the Battle of Trenton were briefly housed in the Old Frame House Tavern on Newtown's State Street.

President Joseph Reed of the Supreme Executive Council realized at once that the transfer would force Pennsylvania to increase the size of its militia. "We foresee very great inconveniences and even dangers arising" from the change, Reed told the state legislature. Reed added: "The British troops amount to one thousand one hundred and eighty-eight. The Germans to one thousand, four hundred, and eighty-seven. A militia guard must also be raised and supported . . . Total to be fed: three thousand seventy-five, besides women and children." Reed calculated that the state would need an additional four hundred militia troops to serve as guards.

Lancaster was well to the south of Pennsylvania's mountainous frontier, where after 1777, Indian attacks had become common, especially during warm weather. British military officers at Fort Niagara, a large post on Lake

Ontario at the mouth of the Niagara River in present-day western New York, often orchestrated these raids, which eased up considerably when winter set in. Defending the frontier had become the responsibility of militia companies organized and funded by the state.

December 1781: Frontier militia guards German POWs

In late 1781, as Indian attacks ceased in the mountains, militia troops posted in frontier counties were sent to Reading to guard the German prisoners. At first, "our company was ordered to Lancaster," but when the men descended the Susquehanna River in boats to Middletown, they found new instructions, Lieutenant Moses Van Campen of the Northumberland County Militia recalled decades later.

"We were ordered to Reading, Berks County," Van Campen said. Two other units had also been ordered to Reading, where "we took charge of the Hessians taken prisoner" at Saratoga, New York, in October 1777.

Van Campen, who himself had spent several days as a prisoner of war before escaping from his Iroquois captors in April 1780, stated in an 1832 affidavit that he spent four months—from "the 1st of December 1781 to the last of March 1782"—in "the guarding of seven hundred Hessians taken prisoners with General Burgoyne."

But this duty was strictly temporary. Governing officials knew that Indian raids would likely resume when the snow melted. By February 28, Colonel Samuel Hunter at Fort Augusta in Sunbury was wondering how soon Van Campen's company would return. William Moore had become president of Pennsylvania's Supreme Executive

Council, and Hunter dashed off a letter to Moore declaring that with "the spring . . . now approaching and the deep snow going off the ground," settlers who had remained on the Northumberland frontier over the winter "expect the cruel hostile visits from their unmerciful enemies early in the spring that they have experienced this three years past."

In Berks County, the militia troops awaited reassignment. As Van Campen reported, "In the latter part of March, just at the opening of the campaign of 1782, the companies that had been stationed during the winter at Reading were ordered back . . . to their respective stations."

The lieutenant said that he "marched at the head of Captain (Thomas) Robinson's company to Northumberland (County)," an overland trek to Fort Augusta, about seventy-five miles to the northwest. The fort was located on the Susquehanna River at Sunbury, and Van Campen halted there for a few days to let his men rest. They were soon sent about thirty miles up the Susquehanna's West Branch "to a place called Muncy, and there (to) rebuild a fort which had been destroyed by the Indians in the year '79."

The men quickly erected a small block house for their stores and then set about constructing a new fort.

In late 1777, when Iroquois warriors began raiding the Susquehanna Valley, landowner Samuel Wallis allowed nearby settlers to assemble on a large tract that he owned on the north shore of the West Branch. The settlers may have even built a small stockade post on the property, which was along a broad bend in the river.

In August 1778, Continental soldiers commanded by Colonel Thomas Hartley had erected Fort Muncy on the Wallis property. Hartley's regiment erected a formidable defense surrounded by a log palisade. But the Continentals abandoned the fort during the summer of 1779, and a war party soon burned it. Although Hunter, the militia commander at Fort Augusta, wanted to rebuild it, he had lacked the troops to do so.

By April 1782, Fort Muncy had still not been rebuilt. The location was so strategic that even Wallis wanted a strong defense there. To reach the Susquehanna settlements from western New York, Iroquois warriors either came down the West Branch in canoes or walked down the Great Shamokin Path that followed the river.

By April 17, Hunter informed General James Potter, now vice president of the Supreme Executive Council, that he had learned Wallis now wanted "to build a fort of stone and lime" on the site, and that he wanted prisoners of war—"a party of Hessians"—to perform the work. "But in the meantime, I give Captain Robinson orders to repair the old fort in the best manner he can at present for his own preservation," Hunter wrote.

Hunter added, "Captain Robinson's headquarters is at Fort Muncy." The situation there might call for the captain to send his rangers across the frontier to guard against Indian attacks rather than have them working on the fort. Even so, "I am certain he does all he can in the ranging way for the good of the county."

Hunter expressed doubt that Robinson's men would make much progress on repairing the fort itself. Iroquois war parties had already struck in the Susquehanna Valley, and these attacks would force the militia to concentrate on protecting the homesteaders, not on repairing the old fort. On April 7, "they took off a woman and four children from

Wyoming," Hunter reported. Seven days later, "a scout of Captain Robinson's men came on fresh tracks of Indians about a mile above Lycoming and followed them up the creek towards Eel Town. I have not heard from them since."

April 1782: War party wipes out militia patrol

In early April, a settler named Andrew Culbertson came to Fort Muncy. He told Captain Robinson and Lieutenant Van Campen that his brother William had had a farm on Bald Eagle Creek, which joined the West Branch about forty miles upriver. Indians had killed his brother there, and Culbertson told the militia officers that he wanted to inspect the farm. The man "was anxious to find an escort up the West Branch ... into the neighborhood of Bald Eagle Creek," Van Campen reported.

Great Island appears in the center of the picture across the Susquehanna River's West Branch near Lock Haven. Bald Eagle Creek, which is not shown, flows along the mountain at left and joins the river a short distance above this location. Lieutenant Van Campen's patrol passed this point as it traveled to the Culbertson farm

Captain Robinson ordered the lieutenant to organize a patrol and accompany Culbertson to the farm. Van Campen set about selecting men for the patrol by testing the marksmanship of Robinson's troops. As the lieutenant's biographer reported decades later:

"Van Campen selected his men according to his usual custom, taking in his hand a small piece of board, on the end of which was a mark of white paper, and standing a few rods in front of his men, who would fire at the mark as it was held up before them, and every man who hit the paper was permitted to have his name enrolled as one of the scout(s)."

A rod is sixteen feet long.

Among the twenty who qualified was Leonard Groninger, the twenty-four-year-old son of German immigrants who had settled in the Buffalo Valley a few miles west of modern-day Lewisburg. The patrol included a goodly mix of German, English, and Irish troops.

As Van Campen started out, Captain Robinson directed him to allow Culbertson adequate time to search the brother's farm, and then "take a circuitous route around the settlements" as he returned to Fort Muncy. This would let Van Campen watch for hostile Indians and to "waylay the Indian paths."

As they left the fort, the militiamen marched along the wagon road that followed the north side of the river. Culbertson and four others in his party went up the West Branch in a small boat. As they headed west, the soldiers had no way of knowing that, northwest of Bald Eagle Creek, Iroquois warriors were descending the West Branch in canoes.

Van Campen told his biographer that when his party reached Great Island opposite the mouth of Bald Eagle Creek, Culbertson and his companions pulled their boat ashore, then accompanied the militia troops as they walked along the creek to the Culbertson farm, a distance of several miles.

It was still light when the warriors reached the bottom of the island. When they spotted Culbertson's boat, they landed, "secured their canoes, and followed the trail of those who had but a short time before left the river," the biographer wrote.

Van Campen said it was getting dark by the time his patrol reached the farm and set up camp for the night. He added that he and his sergeants "placed their sentinels to give the first alarm of the enemy."

The militia troops were wholly unaware that Iroquois warriors had picked up their trail. As Van Campen said years later: "The Indians crept along the path ... and by the morning light, concealed by the bushes, approached very near to the sentries, and burst so unexpectedly upon these that they had only time to run to the camp, crying, 'The Indian! The Indian!' before the savages were in their midst with the tomahawk and scalping knife."

Van Campen said that he "and his men started upon their feet and in a moment were ready for action. The enemy had a warm reception. The combat was at first, from hand to hand, and so well sustained was the resistance that the Indians were obliged to retire, but they came up on all sides, and one after another, Van Campen's men were cut down ..."

The encounter ended with nine of Van Campen's scouts dead. Although Culbertson and several others managed to escape, the warriors captured Van Campen and several other soldiers. The Indians killed most of the wounded prisoners, Van Campen said later. In his biography, Van Campen said there had been as many as eighty-five Indians in the war party.

The captives were taken to the Seneca country in western New York State and eventually turned over to the British at Fort Niagara on Lake Ontario.

Aside from several accounts given by Van Campen, surprisingly little documentation exists to corroborate his version of events. As the militia officer responsible for the region, Colonel Hunter at Fort Augusta often sent reports of Indian raids in Northumberland County to the president. The loss of nearly all of the soldiers in the scout—nine killed and several others taken prisoners—had been a significant event. Still, the many volumes of the Pennsylvania Archives don't contain any reports from Colonel Hunter or any details from anyone else of the April 16 incident at Bald Eagle Creek.

The Archives do, however, contain one document: a list of eleven militiamen who lost their firearms in the fighting. There are other supporting indicators: a 1923 Culbertson family genealogy places Andrew Culbertson in the fight, and a tradition among Leonard Groninger's descendants holds that their ancestor at some point had been a prisoner of the Seneca Indians. Groninger's name appears on the list of men who lost their weapons. The others were: Van Campen, James Dougherty, William McGrady, Ebenezer

Iroquois warriors captured Lieutenant Moses Van Campen of the Northumberland County Militia on the Susquehanna's West Branch, then took him to Fort Niagara, a British post on Lake Ontario. The photo shows part of the fort that is known as the French Castle, built in 1726.

Green, William Miller, Joshua Knapp, Adam Hempleman, Michael Lamb, Jonathan Pray, and Jonathan Burnmell.

The most detailed account of the episode appears in Van Campen's 1842 biography, *Sketches of Border Adventures in the Life and Times of Major Moses Van Campen, a Surviving Soldier of the Revolution.* Its author was Van Campen's grandson, John N. Hubbard.

Two years later, Van Campen appeared before a justice of the peace in Livingston County, New York, and officially requested an increase in the pension he received for his Revolutionary War service. In making the request, he gave this brief description of the defeat he suffered at Bald Eagle Creek: "On the 16th day in April 1782, I was taken prisoner by the Indians and surrendered to the British at Niagara."

Van Campen added that from Fort Niagara, "I was sent to Montreal, from Montreal to Quebec. In the month of November, a British fleet sailed to New York. I was sent with that fleet to New York. In March 1783, I was exchanged and found my company at Northumberland." At war's end, he was discharged from the service.

As for Johannes Schwalm, the Hessian POW remained in Pennsylvania after the Revolution, became a farmer in Schuylkill County, married, and raised a large family. During the American Civil War, some of Schwalm's descendants enlisted in the Union Army.

March 1782

Murder at Killbuck Island

In establishing Pennsylvania during the 1680s, William Penn developed a keen interest in the Lenni Lenape. These native people lived along the Delaware, Schuylkill, and Lehigh rivers in the colony's eastern region.

Penn even learned the Lenape language. "I have made it my business to understand it, that I might not want an Interpreter on any occasion, and I must say that I know not a language spoken in Europe that hath words of more sweetness or greatness in accent and emphasis than theirs."

The proprietor reported that the Lenape word for friend was *netap*, and *pone* meant bread.

Their money was made from certain seashells, from which they fashioned beads. Most beads were white, but some were dark purple or black. "The black is with them as gold; the white, silver," Penn said. "They call it *wampon*."

Penn quickly realized the critical role that *wampon* played in Lenape life. "The justice they have is pecuniary. In case of any wrong . . . be it murther (murder) itself, they atone by feasts and presents of their *wampon*, which is proportioned to the quality of the offense or person injured."

Penn quickly developed a fondness for the Lenape. In turn, the Lenape liked him. Eager to honor the affable

European, they gave him a name in their language. They noted that he used the sharpened end of a quill as a writing instrument, which he said was a pen. The word sounded just like his surname, and the Indians decided to call him "Brother *Miquon*," or Brother Feather.

Born in London in October 1644, William Penn was a vigorous 38 when he arrived in Pennsylvania, a large colony that lay between the Delaware and Susquehanna rivers. King Charles II of England had given him the land to settle a debt the king had owed to Penn's father, Admiral William Penn, who had died in 1670.

Landing at modern-day New Castle, Delaware, in October 1682, the idealistic proprietor packed a lot into his twenty-one-month stay. Putting his stamp on the fledgling colony, he laid out Philadelphia at the confluence of the Delaware and Schuylkill rivers; created a frame of government; presided over civil and criminal cases, including one for witchcraft in February 1683; and established a country estate, Pennsbury Manor, replete with a mansion along the Delaware River.

Before returning to England in August 1684, Penn had become well acquainted with the Lenape Indians whom he saw as "a plain, strong, industrious people;" had obtained considerable information about their way of life; and had purchased land from them. "Some kings have sold, others presented me with several parcels of land," Penn said.

"I have had occasion to be in council with them upon treaties for land," Penn said. All the people in the tribe turned out to witness the purchase. When it was completed, a native orator "made a speech to the Indians in the name of all the . . . kings . . . to tell them what was done."

William Penn

"The pay or presents I made them were not hoarded by the particular owners," but instead were divided among all the villagers, he wrote.

Although Penn himself didn't describe the practice, the Lenape also recorded details of these real estate transactions on special belts and strings made from hundreds, and sometimes thousands, of cylindrical beads fashioned from seashells. Although Penn referred to these beads as *wampon*, most other writers called them *wampum*. The chiefs responsible for them carefully stored them in leather bags.

Perhaps the most famous wampum belt is the one that the Lenape reputedly gave to Penn to commemorate the

Tradition holds that the Lenni Lenape gave this wampum belt to William Penn to commemorate the Treaty of Shackamaxon in or near Philadelphia in 1683.

Treaty of Shackamaxon in or near Philadelphia in June and July of 1683. Penn made some purchases of Lenape land in southeastern Pennsylvania that year. At some point, the Lenape chiefs and Penn met and pledged to live in perpetual peace and friendship. According to legend, the proprietor and Indians met under a great elm tree at Shackamaxon. Penn was quoted as saying, "We meet on the broad pathway of good faith and goodwill; no advantage shall be taken on either side, but all shall be openness and love." Tamanend, the Lenape head chief, replied: "We will live in love with William Penn and his children as long as the creeks and rivers run, and while the sun, moon, and stars endure."

The wampum belt that tradition says the Lenape made to mark the occasion has survived. It is eighteen rows wide and fashioned mainly from white wampum beads. It depicts two men—a Native American and a European—holding hands as they stand side by side.

William Penn left Pennsylvania for the last time in November 1701. Seventy years later, the Lenape still used the wampum records of these and other land sales and treaties as tools to remember their tribal history. "Between the years 1770 and 1780, they could relate very minutely what had passed between William Penn and their forefathers, at their first meeting and afterward," said John Heckewelder, a Moravian missionary who not only lived among these Indians for thirty years but also spoke their language fluently.

By 1770, few Lenape remained along the Delaware River. Most had moved to the Ohio River Valley, where they became known as the Delaware Indians.

The missionary said that once or twice a year, chiefs

The Reverend John Heckewelder, Moravian missionary to the Delaware Indians

and other Delaware leaders withdrew from their villages and met at a specific spot in the woods to review the tribal records. The Delawares did this for "the purpose of refreshing their own memories, and of instructing one or more of their most capable and promising young men in these matters," Heckewelder said.

The missionary described such a session: "There, on a large piece of bark or on a blanket, all the documents are laid out in . . . order." These documents were mainly "belts or strings of wampum," but by this time, the records also included documents written in English on paper or parchment. "When any written documents were produced, they would request one or the other of the missionaries to attend, to read and interpret them," the missionary said.

Heckewelder described the review process. A knowledgeable native speaker, "already . . . trained up to the business, rises, and in an audible voice delivers, with the gravity that the subject requires, the contents, sentence after sentence, until he has finished the whole on one subject," Heckewelder said. "Belts and strings, when done with by the speaker, are again handed to the chief, who puts them up carefully in the speech-bag or pouch."

The Delaware chief who had custody of the tribal records during part of the early 1770s was an elderly man named Netawatwees, who was also known as Newcomer. He had grown up in eastern Pennsylvania and had been among the many Delawares evicted from the Lenape homeland by William Penn's sons and the Iroquois Indians in 1742 in the aftermath of the Walking Purchase of 1737.

"It was with this chief that I saw at different times the speeches of William Penn and his successors," the missionary wrote. ". . . Of William Penn, whom he personally had known, he spoke respectfully."

In October 1776, when Newcomer was nearly ninety, he died while attending a treaty with the Americans at Pittsburgh. Two years later, Newcomer's successor, Captain White Eyes, died suddenly, and a chief named Gelelemend—also known as Killbuck Junior—became king of the Ohio Delawares. This gave Gelelemend custody of the tribal records.

As the war progressed, the Delawares split into factions. Some sided with the British, others with the Americans, and many wanted to remain neutral. In time, the conflict turned bitter. As Killbuck explained in a 1788 letter, "at the beginning of the war with Great Britain," he had enjoyed "much favor with the Delaware Indians and for some time prevented them from committing any outrage upon the inhabitants of the United States."

Colonel Daniel Brodhead, the commander at Fort Pitt, and other American military officers actively encouraged

Constructed in 1764, this blockhouse was part of Fort Pitt, an American post at Pittsburgh during the Revolutionary War. Library of Congress photo.

the Delawares to fight against the pro-British Indians. Their leaders received military commissions. By early 1781, Killbuck held the rank of colonel.

February 1781: Delawares switch sides

Killbuck was at Fort Pitt in February 1781, when an influential war chief, Captain Pipe, persuaded the Delawares at Goschocking, a Delaware town about a hundred-twenty miles west of Pittsburgh at present-day Coshocton, Ohio, to abandon the alliance they had made with the Americans several years earlier and to join the British.

As he returned to Ohio, Killbuck learned that many Delawares had changed sides and intended to take up the hatchet against the Americans "immediately at the change of this moon." Rather than return to Goschocking, the chief stopped at Salem, a Moravian mission some thirty miles east of the Delaware village. The mission was along the Muskingum River, known now as the Tuscarawas. Heckewelder was the missionary there, and on February 26, he helped Killbuck write a letter to Colonel Brodhead at Fort Pitt that warned of the Delawares' change of heart.

"The men are getting ready to go and fight you," Killbuck said. The pro-British warriors intended "first to destroy all the Delawares that are friends to the (United) States, and then to proceed to Beaver Creek and Fort Pitt." An American post, Fort McIntosh, stood on the Ohio at the mouth of Beaver Creek some thirty miles below Pittsburgh.

In late April, Brodhead led a force of about three hundred men into Ohio and attacked Goschocking. They met little opposition, burned the town, and destroyed a nearby village called Indaochaie before returning to Fort Pitt.

Colonel Brodhead credited Killbuck with an assist. "Captain Killbuck and Captain Luzerne, upon hearing of our troops being on the Muskingum, immediately pursued the warriors, killed one of their greatest villains and brought his scalp to me," Brodhead wrote in informing Joseph Reed, president of the Pennsylvania Supreme Executive Council, about his attacks on the hostile towns.

Moravian missionaries had established three missions—Salem, Gnadenhutten, and Shonbrun—along the present-day Tuscarawas River. About ninety miles due west of Pittsburgh, the missions were agricultural. Native converts learned European-style farming and farm-related trades such as barrel making.

Killbuck had been staying at the Salem mission during this time because one morning soon after Brodhead's expedition, eighty enemy Delawares suddenly appeared at the mission. "Having surrounded the town completely, (they) hailed the inhabitants to deliver into their hands the chief Gelelemend, alias Killbuck, with the other chiefs and counselors, whom they must have either alive or dead," Heckewelder reported.

Told that all had gone to Pittsburgh and that none were in Salem, "they then searched every house, stable and cellar," Heckewelder wrote. The warriors eventually left but not before Pachgantschihilas, described by Heckewelder as "the head war chief of the Delaware Nation," addressed the mission Indians. He encouraged them to leave the mission and follow him to a much safer location.

The chief noted that Salem was located between the pro-British Indians living along Lake Erie to the north and the Pennsylvania and Virginia settlements to the south. He asked rhetorically, "Do you not live in the very road the contending parties pass over when they go to fight each other? Have you not discovered the footsteps of the long knives, almost within sight of your towns, and seen the smoke arising from their camps? Should not this be sufficient warning to you?"

The chief warned them bluntly: "If you stay where you now are, one day or the other, the long knives will in their usual way speak fine words to you and at the same time murder you!"

Shortly after the incident involving Pachgantschihilas, Killbuck fled to Pittsburgh permanently. As the pro-British chiefs became powerful in the tribe, ". . . I soon lost my influence and popularity and was obliged with my family to run away and take refuge in the garrison at Fort Pitt," the chief said after the war.

At first, Killbuck and the warriors who remained loyal to him had lived in Pittsburgh, but "some short time after my arrival at Fort Pitt, the commanding officer fixed me and my family on a small island supposed to contain about twenty acres or thereabouts."

Smoky Island was less than a quarter of a mile long. As Pittsburgh lawyer Hugh H. Brackenridge described it in 1786: "At the distance of about four or five hundred yards from the head of the Ohio is a small island, lying to the northwest side of the (Allegheny) river, at the distance of about seventy yards from the shore. It is covered with wood, and at the lowest point is a lofty hill, famous for the number of wild turkeys which inhabit it."

Details about Killbuck's encampment on the island are sketchy. After the war, the chief himself said that the island was "nearly opposite the garrison in the Allegheny River, of which I cleared about ten acres, which has supplied my small family in bread." It isn't known whether the Indians lived in wigwams, which were circular houses supported by a framework of saplings and covered by sheets of bark, or in one-room log cabins constructed by soldiers from Fort Pitt or residents of Pittsburgh. It is possible that Killbuck's settlement consisted of a combination of cabins and wigwams. The Delaware men likely fished in the river to supplement the corn and other crops the women raised on the farm.

The warriors who accompanied Killbuck to the island included a Delaware named Nanowland. He had served with distinction during Brodhead's 1781 raid against the pro-British Delawares at Goshocking. Nanowland had worked closely with Captain Samuel Brady, a well-known frontier scout who belonged to a Pennsylvania regiment in the Continental Army.

Brodhead himself singled out one of the Delawares for special recognition. "I certify that in consequence of the faithful service of Captain Wilson (an Indian), as well as to encourage him to be active in future expeditions and detachments, I did, last spring, make him a present of a small black horse, belonging to the United States," the colonel wrote at Fort Pitt on November 18, 1781.

A third was Big Cat, whose Delaware name, Machingue Puschiis, meant "the large cat," according to Heckewelder. The missionary knew him and described him as "an able counselor" who had "assisted William Henry Killbuck faithfully in maintaining the nation at peace."

The Ohio frontier remained a dangerous place to live. Recognizing this, the new commander at Fort Pitt, Brigadier General William Irvine, in early 1782 stationed an officer's guard on Smoky Island, which was becoming known as Killbuck Island, providing security for these Delawares.

September 1781: Mission Indians uprooted

In September 1781, the pro-British Delawares forced the Christian Indians and their Moravian missionaries to abandon the mission towns along the Tuscarawas and move to Sandusky, a native town on Lake Erie. The

Christian Indians at the Moravian missions in Ohio lived in cabins such as this one, a reconstruction at Schoenbrunn Village, a recreated mission at New Philadelphia, Ohio. (Photo courtesy of Robert B. Swift.)

warriors compelled the Christian Indians to abandon their livestock and "at least three hundred acres of corn, ripe for harvesting, exclusive of a great quantity of old corn, potatoes, turnips, (and) cabbages," Heckewelder said.

Late in the winter of 1781-1782, with food supplies running low at Sandusky, the Christian Indians returned to the Moravian towns to harvest corn they had left in the fields.

During this time, pro-British warriors raided the white settlements south of Pittsburgh in present-day Washington

County. Four of these warriors stopped at Gnadenhutten on their way back to Sandusky. They told the mission Indians about the raids and warned them "that the white people. . . . might make up a party and pursue them." The warriors "advised them to be on their guard," and to leave "as soon as possible." The Moravian Indians thought this over and decided they weren't in any danger. After all, "they were not the hostile, but the Christian Indians."

By early March, "they had already secured as much corn as they thought would serve them for the season," and were preparing to return to Sandusky. Heckewelder said. "On the day our Indians were bundling up their packs, intending to set off on the next morning, a party of between one and two hundred white people from the Ohio settlements made their appearance at Gnadenhutten," he said.

These men, many of them members of the Washington County Militia, had decided to retaliate against the raids by riding into the Indian territory north of the Ohio River and destroying the missions. They suspected that Indians living there provided housing and food for warriors headed to and returning from the white settlements. Burning the towns would prevent enemy war parties from using them "as a shelter and base of operations," Boyd Crumrine said in his 1882 *History of Washington County, Pennsylvania.*

To accomplish this, Colonel James Marshall called out the county militia: "The force, which consisted of about one hundred and sixty men, . . . and all, or very nearly all, of whom were mounted, was placed under command of Colonel David Williamson. It left the county on the 3rd of March, and in the morning of the 4th crossed the Ohio

River to the Mingo Bottom, which was on the western bank of the stream, about two and a half miles below the present town of Steubenville (Ohio)," Crumrine said.

Led by Colonel Williamson, the men rode into Gnadenhutten on the morning of March 7. The Indian Jacob, who survived the ensuing massacre, later told Heckewelder how the attack had begun.

Jacob was about a hundred and fifty yards from the town, tying up sacks of corn near the riverbank when the horsemen rode up. He said that he "saw the party coming on, between himself and the Tuscarawas, and so near him that . . . he might have seen the black in their eyes, had they looked in the direction where he was standing. . . . He was about hailing them, when to his astonishment, they at that instant shot at one of the (Moravian) brethren who was just crossing the river in a canoe to go to the cornfield, and who, dropping down at the shot, Jacob supposed him to be killed."

Jacob promptly fled into the forest and hid.

The Indians at the mission and in nearby cornfields hadn't heard the gunshot, because Williamson's men quickly rounded them up and disarmed them. As mission Indians, they had few weapons, were quickly taken prisoner, and confined in log houses at the mission. When the militiamen learned there were also Christian Indians nearby at the Salem mission, they sent for them, professing friendship. When the Salem converts arrived at Gnadenhutten, they quickly realized they had been deceived. "The Gnadenhutten brethren, sisters, and children were already confined," Heckewelder wrote.

The Pennsylvanians quickly imprisoned the Indians from Salem, confining them in houses in which the Gnadenhutten congregation had lived.

Eventually, the Indians were brought out of the houses one by one, and the militiamen began killing them. "One of the party now taking up a cooper's mallet, which lay in the house—the owner being a cooper" and ". . . he began with (a convert named) Abraham, and continued knocking down one after the other until he had counted fourteen that he had killed with his own hands," Heckewelder said.

The murders completed, the Pennsylvanians "set fire to the houses (and) they went off, shouting and yelling, on having been so victorious," Heckewelder wrote.

"The number of Christian Indians murdered by these miscreants exceeded ninety. All of whom, except four, were killed in the slaughter houses," the missionary reported. The four included "Jacob, who had been shot down in the canoe, and two young brethren, Paul and Anthony, who . . . were shot down . . . whilst attempting to escape. Of the above number, sixty-two were grown persons, one-third of whom were women. The remaining thirty-four were children."

News of the killings swept across the frontier. At Fort Pitt, General Irvine put the number of militia troops at "about three hundred" men. In an April 20 letter to General Washington, Irvine reported that the militia "had just returned from the Moravian towns, where they found about ninety men, women, and children, all of whom they put to death."

In an April 12 letter to his wife, Irvine said the Pennsylvanians had done the killing "in cool blood, having deliberated three days, during which time they were industrious in collecting all (Indian) hands into their churches (they had embraced Christianity) where they fell on, while they were singing hymns, and killed the whole. Many children were killed in their wretched mothers' arms."

Heckewelder's account of the massacre was understandably colored by his long-term role as a missionary to these Indians. Although he wasn't present when the murders took place, he was living in Ohio, and soon after the event, obtained eyewitness accounts from Indians who had survived.

General Irvine, as the Continental Army's commanding officer at Fort Pitt, provided a more objective account. Although the general received—and forwarded to the president of Pennsylvania—reports of the Gnaddenhutten campaign from Colonel Williamson and Colonel Marshall, these records appear to have been lost.

Irvine contended that facts were difficult to acquire. "Every intelligent person whom I have conversed with on the subject are of the opinion that it will be almost impossible ever to obtain a just account of the conduct of the militia at Muskingum," Irvine told William Moore, president of the Supreme Executive Council in a May letter.

"No man can give any account except some of the party themselves," Irvine said. "If, therefore, an inquiry should appear serious, they are not obliged, nor will they give evidence. For this and other reasons, I am of opinion further inquiry into the matter will not only be fruitless but, in the end, may be attended with disagreeable consequences."

Moore replied that Irvine's letters—along "with the representations made by Colonel Williamson and Colonel Marshall—have been read in Council and shall be immediately laid before Congress as a matter of high importance..."

Moore requested "that you will continue your inquiries on this subject and transmit us such information from time to time, as may come to your knowledge tending to elucidate this dark transaction."

No formal investigations or prosecutions ever took place. The Christian Indians had been falsely accused, Heckewelder charged in his 1820 book, *History of the Mission of the United Brethren Among the Delaware and Mohegan Indians*. "... Far from their joining in the war, they followed their agricultural pursuit, the whole time they lived on the Muskingum (present-day Tuscarawas)."

The mission Indians had "lived in peace together until their settlements were broken up by a host of Indian warriors from the side of the British, their property destroyed, their ministers taken prisoners; and with themselves forcibly carried ... off to the barren plains of Upper Sandusky." Despite the efforts of the pro-British Delawares, these Christian Indians, who had become pacifists, "could not be induced to join in the war, and turn out to fight the American people." Heckewelder said.

March 1782: Vigilantes attack Killbuck Island

Gunfire coming from Killbuck Island in the Allegheny River across from Fort Pitt shattered the morning quiet of Sunday, March 24.

Killbuck and the other pro-American Delawares suddenly realized they were being attacked. Armed whites forded the river on horseback, rode onto the island, and commenced shooting even though, as a Pittsburgh lawyer said later, their targets were "friendly Indians . . . under the protection of the (Fort Pitt) garrison."

The raiders killed Nanowland and Captain Wilson, captured the soldiers that General Irvine had placed on the island to guard Killbuck's people, and forced Killbuck and the others to flee. Killbuck "saved his life only by taking to the river and swimming across to the point or town, leaving all his property behind," Heckewelder said later.

Although Big Cat "narrowly escaped," the dead included a "promising young Delaware chief," Heckewelder said.

According to Hugh H. Brackenridge, the Pittsburgh lawyer, the riders "had come from the Chartiers, a settlement south of the Monongahela, in the neighborhood of this town."

Among the dead were several Delawares "that had been of essential service to the whites in expeditions against Indian towns, and on scouting parties in case of attacks upon the settlements," Brackenridge said. In particular, Captain Wilson's death "was much regretted by the garrison," Brackenridge reported.

In an April 12 letter, Irvine irately reported that as they invaded the island, the riders "made prisoners of a guard of Continental troops."

In a second letter, this one to General Washington on April 20, nearly a month after the attack, Irvine said, "There was an officer's guard on the Island at the same time, but he (the officer) either did not do his duty, or his men connived at the thing, which I am not yet able to ascertain."

The attackers had "killed two who had captains' commissions in our service, and several others," Irvine told Washington. "The remainder effected their escape into the fort, except two who ran to the woods, and have not since been heard off."

One of the two presumably was Big Cat. According to Heckewelder, the man retreated deep into Indian territory. The raid marked the end of Big Cat's affection for Americans, "from that time not trusting any more to their pretended friendship," the missionary said.

Nearly a month after the raid, several Delawares who had survived the attack insisted on staying at Fort Pitt even though Irvine didn't want them at his post. "The few remaining Indians, chiefly women, and children, are exceeding troublesome to us, as they dare not stir out of the fort," Irvine told Washington. "Not one of the warriors will even venture on a reconnoitering party."

Irvine wanted the Indians removed from Fort Pitt as quickly as possible. "I think they would be better in some more interior part of the country where they could be both cheaper fed and clothed," he said. ". . . It is not only inconvenient but improper to have them among the troops who are, without them, crowded in dirty bad barracks."

Irvine added, "I beg your Excellency's instructions how to dispose of them."

Despite Irvine's opposition, Killbuck and his Delawares remained in the vicinity of Pittsburgh for an extended time. They were still there in September 1783, long after the war had shifted from the battlefield to the peace table. That's when a German traveler, Johann D. Schoepf, stopped at Fort Pitt and Pittsburgh, which had become a village "on the eastern bank of the Monongahela (River) some three hundred yards from the fort." There were "perhaps sixty wooden houses and cabins, in which live something more than a hundred families . . . The first stone house was built this summer."

When Schoepf learned that some Delaware Indians "were living at this time close by the fort," he went to see them. "Accompanied by an officer of the garrison I visited their chief, Colonel Killbuck," Schoepf wrote in his 1788 two-volume work, *Travels in the Confederation (1783-1784)*. He didn't reveal the location of Killbuck's village, so it's not known whether the Delawares had returned to the island or were living on the mainland.

Killbuck, born in 1737 in eastern Pennsylvania along the Lehigh River north of modern-day Allentown, was in his mid-forties when Schoepf showed up. "The colonel, whom we found in a dirty and ragged shirt, had the day before returned from a long hunt, and was now refreshing himself with drink," the German said. "He spoke a broken English."

To Schoepf's surprise, Killbuck disclosed that his son was attending college in New Jersey" "at the expense of the Congress . . . at Princeton" — "and brought out with pride a few letters written to him . . ."

Schoepf reported that the Indians were living in huts rather than cabins or houses. "Their wigwams," he said, "were contrived, merely for summer, of poles and the bark of trees. They would build better, they said, against the winter. There were about a dozen huts.

"Their beds of bear-skins were spread on the ground about the fire, which in every case was burning in the middle. The flesh-pot is never taken from the fire except to be emptied and again filled, for they are always eating and are bound by no fixed times. The walls of all the huts were hung with bones, corn stalks, and dried venison . . ."

One of the men Schoepf met was "Captain (Joseph) White Eye(s) who was strutting about wrapped in a checkered blanket, with rings in his nose and his ears, and sumptuously adorned with colored streaks down his face."

The German's arrival didn't disrupt domestic activity underway in the village.

"A young, well-formed, copper-brown squaw was beating maize in a wooden trough before one of the huts," Schoepf reported. "Her entire costume consisted of a tight petticoat of blue cloth hardly reaching to the knees . . . Her straight black hair hung loose over the shoulders; her cheeks and forehead (were) nicely daubed in red. She seemed very well content with the society of . . . a brisk young fellow who except for two rags appropriately disposed was quite as naked . . . Other women were occupied in pleating baskets (and) shelling corn."

Schoepf, who had come to North America as a surgeon in a German regiment in 1777, didn't mention the military service that Killbuck and other Delaware men had performed for the Americans during the war. Instead, he noted, "The Indians are generally hated here quite as much as they are pretty well throughout America."

Killbuck Island no longer exists. Flooding on the Allegheny River destroyed it during the 1800s. The late Pittsburgh historian Margaret Pearson Bothwell reported in a 1961 article, "Killbuck and Killbuck Island," that a great flood carried off much of the island in 1832. The freshet left only "a small part which was carried off by another flood about ten years thereafter." She said that her source was the text of an 1873 law enacted by the Pennsylvania Legislature.

Although American authorities never prosecuted anyone for the murders of the Christian Indians, pro-British Delawares avenged the killings. In June 1782, they executed ten American prisoners captured following a Washington County Militia raid against Sandusky, the native town on Lake Erie. A two-day battle ended with the militia in a panicky retreat. The Indians caught Colonel William Crawford, who led the expedition, and ten others. "Captain Pipe ordered them to be burned at the stake," according to the late historian C. Hale Sipe.

As General Irvine later reported to Washington, Crawford "was burned and tortured in every manner they could invent." Dr. John Knight, a surgeon, managed to escape. The Delawares had told Knight that they would deal harshly with future American captives: "Not a single soul should in future escape torture, and (they) gave as a reason for this conduct the Moravian affair."

Long after the Revolutionary War, his missionary service ended, John Heckewelder wrote about the Delawares and the many years he spent among them. He lamented that among the property lost by Killbuck in the 1782 raid on the island "was the bag containing all the wampum speeches and written documents of William Penn and his successors for a great number of years, which had for so long a time been carefully preserved by them, but now had fallen into the hands of a murdering band of white savages."

The men who raided Killbuck Island and murdered the Delawares were never brought to justice. The whereabouts of the leather bag and the wampum, paper and parchment documents it contained remains a mystery.

Selective Bibliography

Books

Colonial Records of Pennsylvania. Vol. XI. Harrisburg, PA: Theo. Fenn & Co., 1852.

Curwen, Samuel. *The Journal and Letters of Samuel Curwen, an American in England from 1775 to 1783.* Fourth edition. Boston: Little, Brown and Co., 1864.

Denny, Ebenezer. *Military Journal of Major Ebenezer Denny, An Officer in the Revolutionary and Indian Wars.* Philadelphia: J. B. Lippincott & Co., 1859.

du Motier, Gilbert, Marquis de La Fayette. *Memoirs, Correspondence, and Manuscripts of General Lafayette, Published by His Family.* Vol. I. New York and London: Saunders and Otley, 1837.

Donehoo, George P. *Indian Villages and Place Names in Pennsylvania.* Baltimore: Gateway Press Inc., 1995.

Heckewelder, John. *An Account of the History, Manners, and Customs of the Indian Nations, Who Once Inhabited Pennsylvania and the Neighboring States.* Philadelphia: Publication Fund of the Historical Society of Pennsylvania, 1876. (Reprint edition by Arno Press Inc., 1971)

Heckewelder, John. *A Narrative of the Mission of the United Brethren Among the Delaware and Mohegan Indians.* Philadelphia: McCarty & Davis, 1820.

Hubbard, John N. *Sketches of Border Adventures in the Life and Times of Major Moses Van Campen, a Surviving Soldier of the Revolution, by his Grandson, John N. Hubbard.* Bath, NY: R. L. Underhill & Co., 1842.

Johnston, Henry P. *The Yorktown Campaign and the Surrender of Cornwallis 1781.* New York: Harper & Brothers, 1881

Moser, G. Paul, editor. *Johannes Schwalm The Hessian.* Millville, Pa.: Precision Printers Inc., 1976.
Pennsylvania Archives, Vol. V. Edited by Samuel Hazard. Philadelphia: Joseph Severns & Co., 1853.
———. Vol. VII. Edited by Samuel Hazard. Philadelphia: Joseph Severns & Co., 1853.
———. Vol. IX. Edited by Samuel Hazard. Philadelphia: Joseph Severns & Co., 1854.
———. Second Series. Vol. XV. Edited by William H. Egle. Harrisburg: E.K. Meyers, State Printer, 1890.
———. Fifth Series. Vol. III. Edited by Thomas L. Montgomery. Harrisburg: Harrisburg Publishing Company, State Printer, 1906.
The Pennsylvania Magazine of History and Biography. Vol. V. Philadelphia: The Historical Society of Pennsylvania, 1881.
Scheer, George F., and Rankin, Hugh F. *Rebels and Redcoats: The American Revolution Through the Eyes of Those That Fought and Lived It.* New York: The World Publishing Co., 1957.
Schoepf, Johann D. *Travels in the Confederation (1783-1784).* Ed. & trans. Alfred J. Morrison. Philadelphia: William J. Campbell, 1911.
Wallace, Paul A. W. *Indian Paths of Pennsylvania.* Harrisburg: Pennsylvania Historical and Museum Commission, 1971.
Weslager, C.A. *The Delaware Indians.* New Brunswick: Rutgers University Press, 1972.

Internet resources:

Dictionary.com @ https://www.dictionary.com/
Founders Online @ https://founders.archives.gov/
Google maps @ https://www.google.com/maps/
Internet Archive @ https://archive.org/

About the Author

John L. Moore of Northumberland is a writer and storyteller whose subjects deal with real people and actual events in Pennsylvania history.

Murder on Killbuck Island is the fifth book in his Revolutionary Pennsylvania Series, which tells the stories of Pennsylvania and Pennsylvanians caught up in the American Revolutionary War. It is a companion to *Tories, Terror, and Tea* (2017); *Scorched Earth: General Sullivan and the Senecas* (2018); *1780: Year of Revenge* (2019); and *Against the Ice: The Story of December 1776* (2020).

Murder on Killbuck Island is the author's thirteenth non-fiction book. Sunbury Press Inc. published the eight non-fiction books in Moore's Frontier Pennsylvania Series in 2014.

Mr. Moore has participated in several archaeological excavations of Native American sites. These include the Village of Nain in Bethlehem, Pa.; the City Island project in Harrisburg, Pa., conducted by the Pennsylvania Historical and Museum Commission; a Bloomsburg University dig in 1999 at a Native American site near Nescopeck, Pa.; and a 1963 excavation of the New Jersey State Museum along the Delaware River north of Worthington State Forest.

Mr. Moore's 46-year newspaper career (1966-2012) included stints as a reporter for The Wall Street Journal; as managing editor of The Sentinel at Lewistown, Pa.; as editorial page editor, city editor and managing editor of The Daily Item in Sunbury, and as editor of the Eastern Pennsylvania Business Journal in Bethlehem, Pa. He was also a Harrisburg correspondent for Ottaway Newspapers in the early 1970s.

A professional storyteller, Moore specializes in historically accurate stories about Pennsylvanians. Wearing 18th century-style clothing, he often appears in the persona of Susquehanna Jack.

For information about Mr. Moore's storytelling programs and books, please contact:

John L. Moore
552 Queen Street
Northumberland, Pa. 17857
Telephone (570) 473-9803
Email: tomahawks1756@gmail.com

www.ingramcontent.com/pod-product-compliance
Lightning Source LLC
Chambersburg PA
CBHW020009050426
42450CB00005B/378